PIANO | VOCAL | GUITAR ▪ AUDIO

VOLUME 5

CONTENTS

To access audio visit:
www.halleonard.com/mylibrary

Enter Code
4679-6636-6271-5157

WONDERLAND MUSIC COMPANY, INC.
WALT DISNEY MUSIC COMPANY

ISBN 978-0-634-06905-5

DISTRIBUTED BY

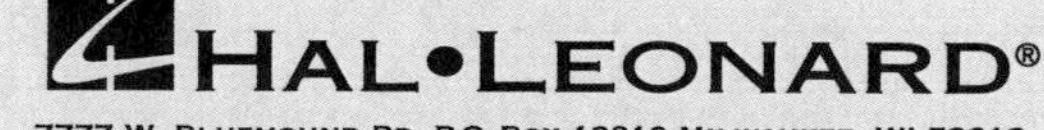

7777 W. BLUEMOUND RD. P.O. BOX 13819 MILWAUKEE, WI 53213

In Australia Contact:
Hal Leonard Australia Pty. Ltd.
4 Lentara Court
Cheltenham, Victoria, 3192 Australia
Email: ausadmin@halleonard.com.au

Visit Hal Leonard Online at
www.halleonard.com

BEAUTY AND THE BEAST

from Walt Disney's BEAUTY AND THE BEAST

Music by ALAN MENKEN
Lyrics by HOWARD ASHMAN

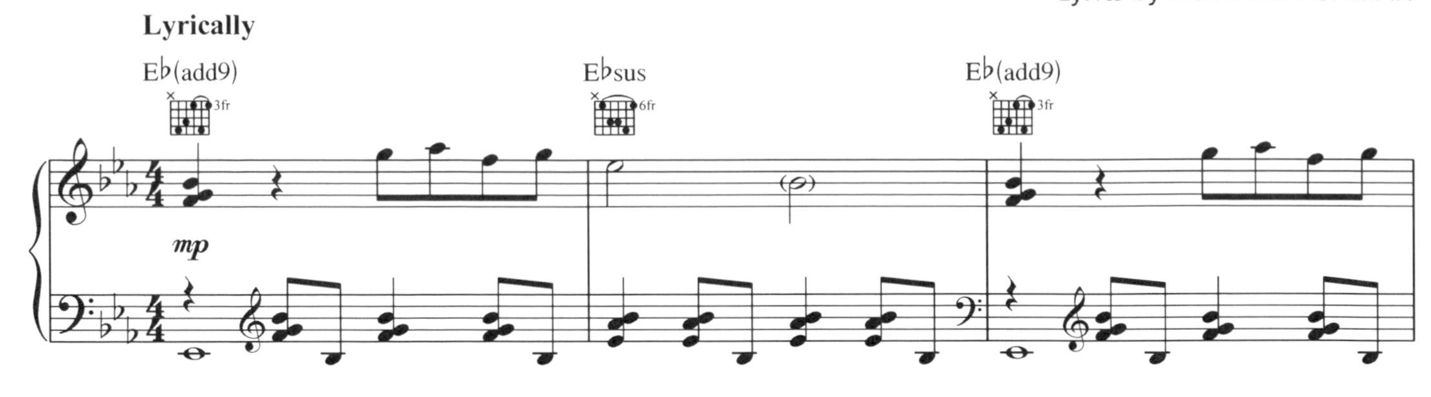

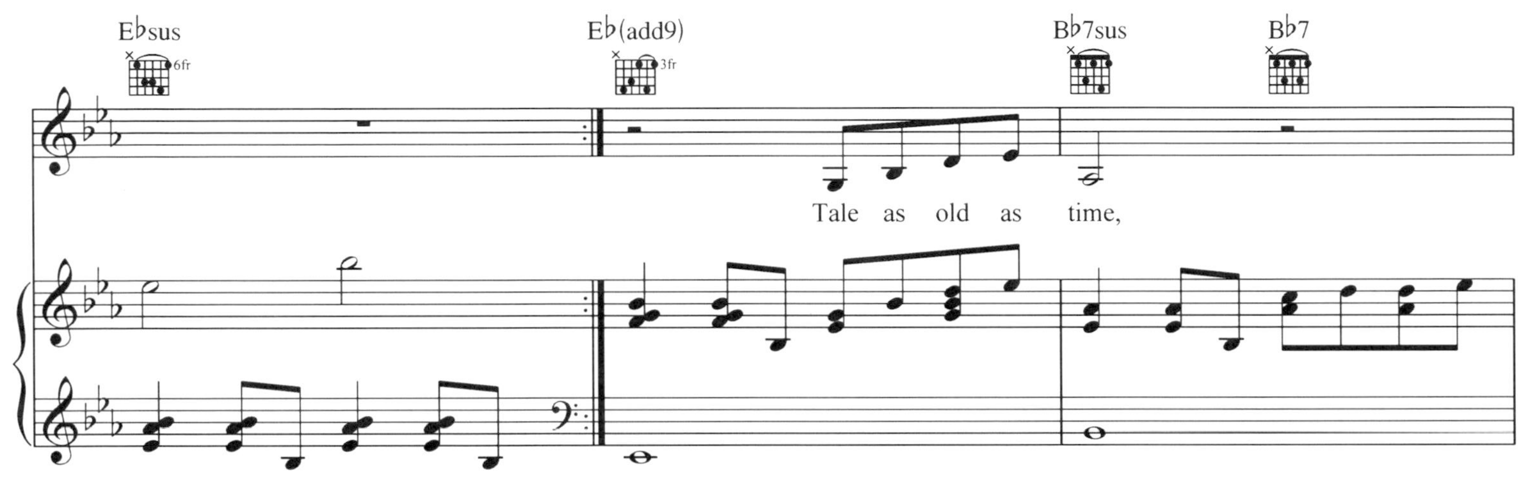

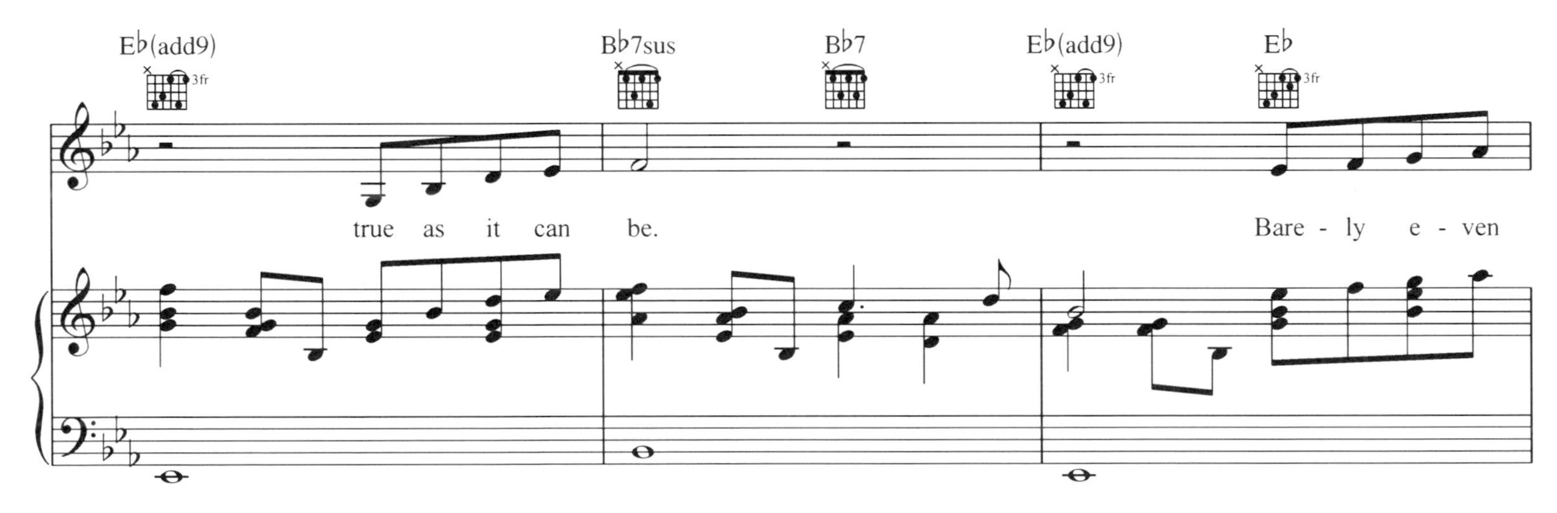

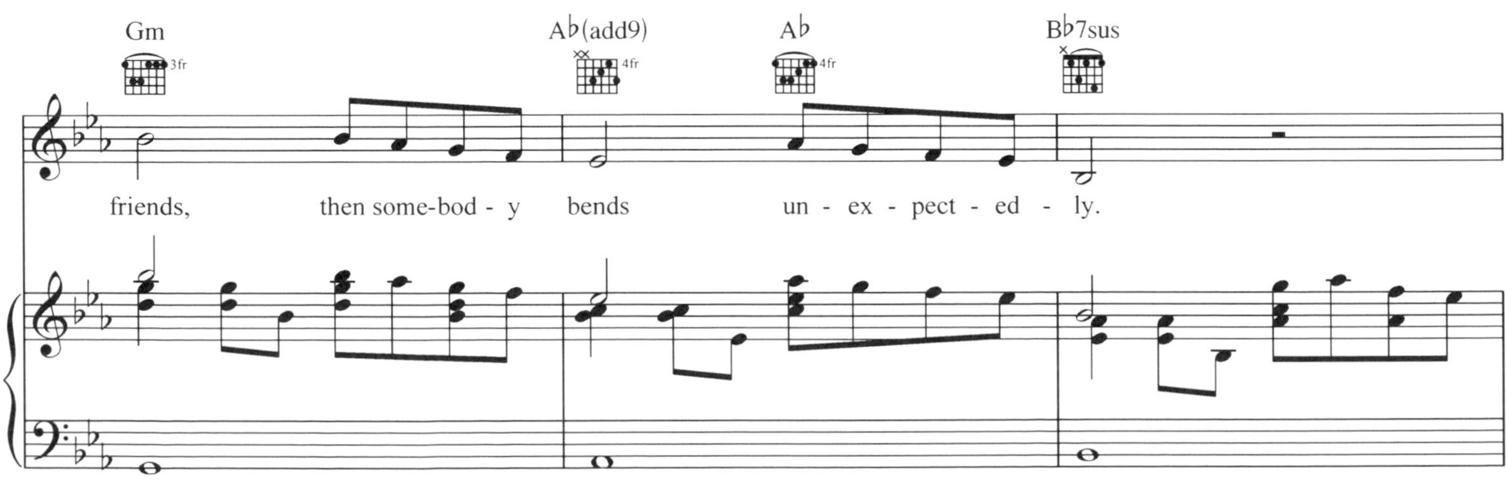

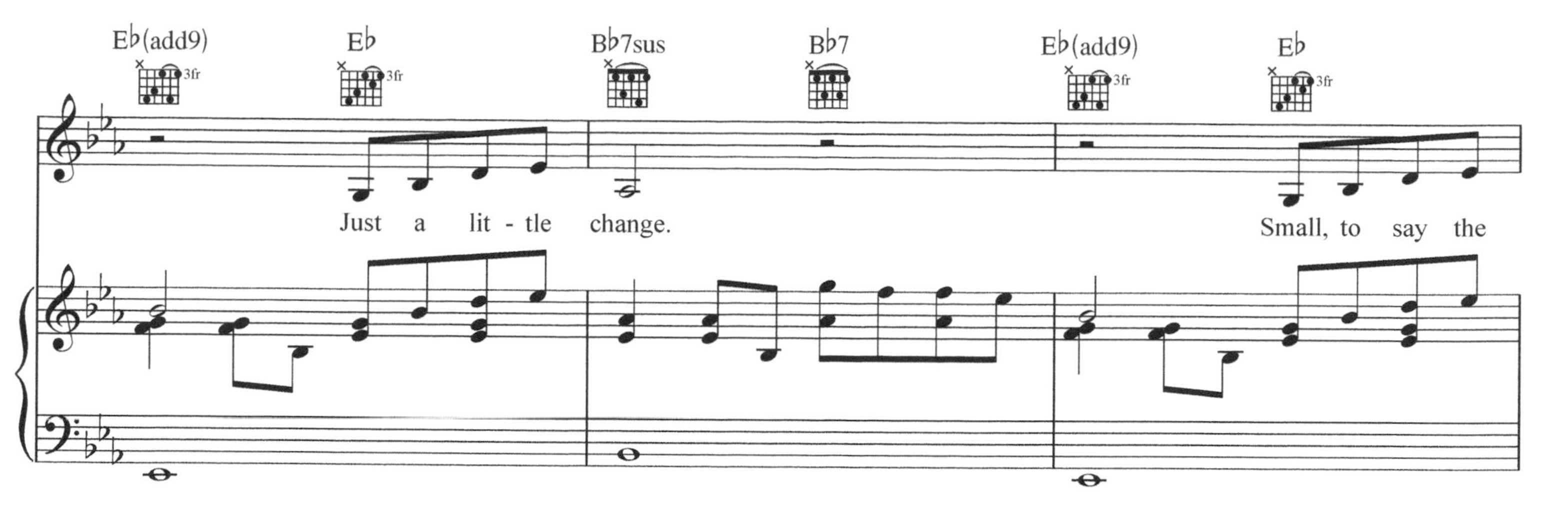
E♭(add9)
E♭
B♭7sus
B♭7
E♭(add9)
E♭
Just a lit - tle change.
Small, to say the

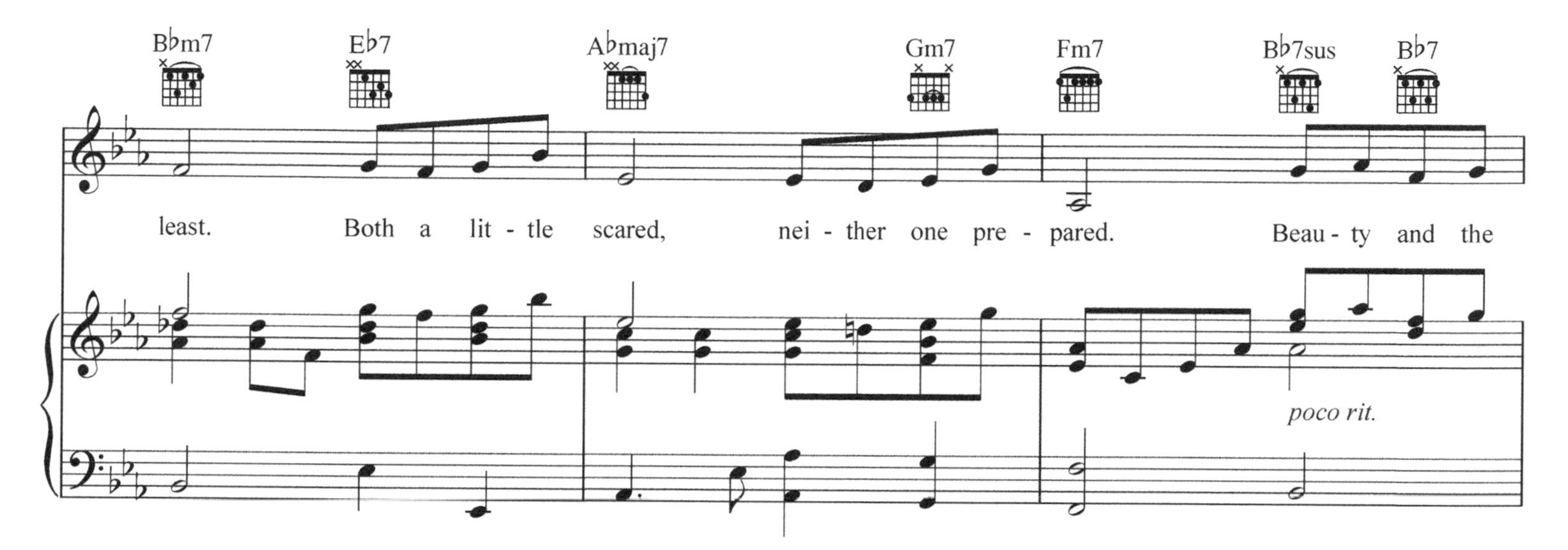
B♭m7
E♭7
A♭maj7
Gm7
Fm7
B♭7sus
B♭7
least. Both a lit - tle scared, nei - ther one pre - pared. Beau - ty and the
poco rit.

E♭(add9)
B♭7sus
Gm
Beast. Ev - er just the same.
a tempo
mf

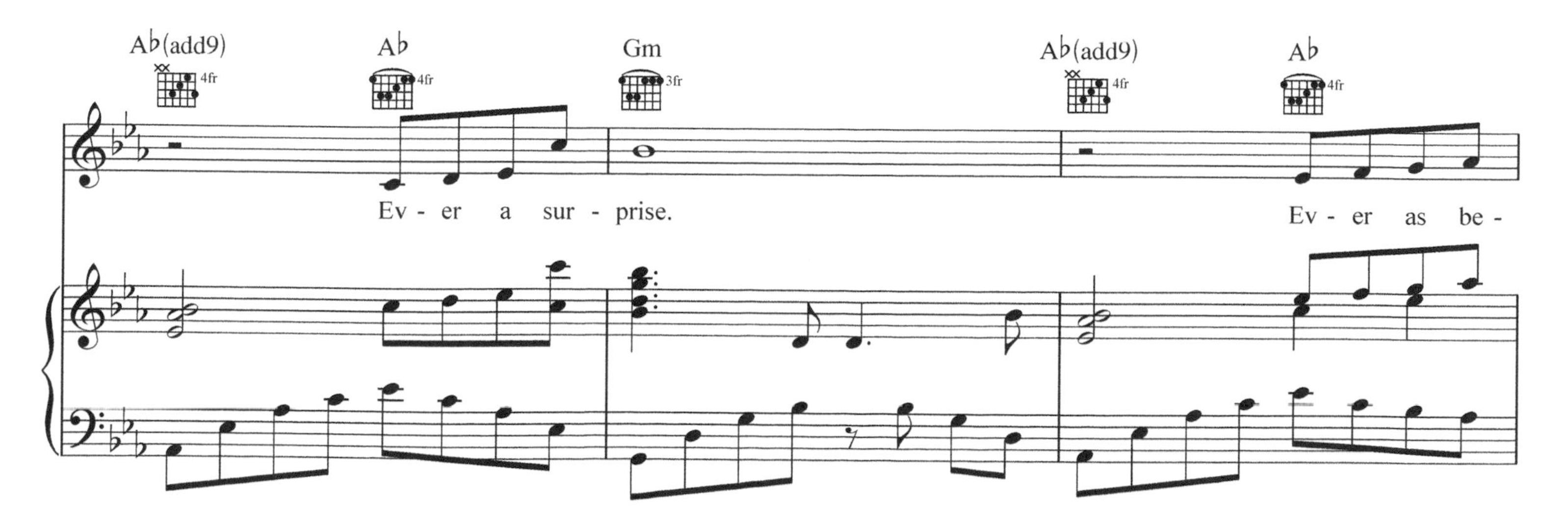
A♭(add9)
A♭
Gm
A♭(add9)
A♭
Ev - er a sur - prise. Ev - er as be -

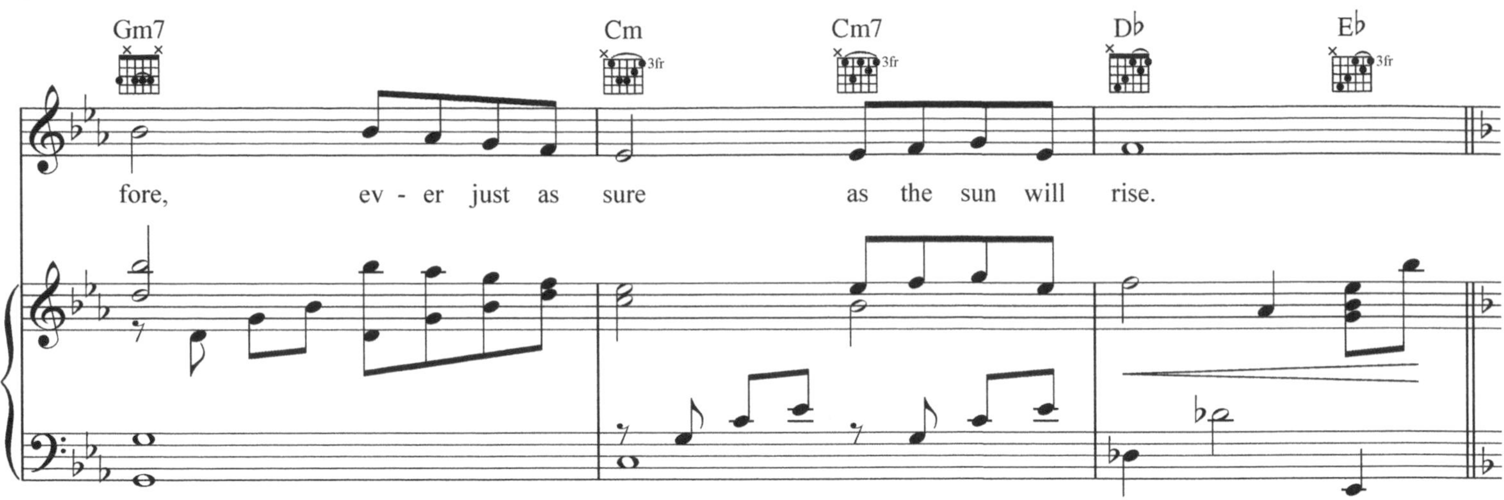
Gm7
Cm
Cm7
3fr
D♭
E♭
fore, ev - er just as sure as the sun will rise.

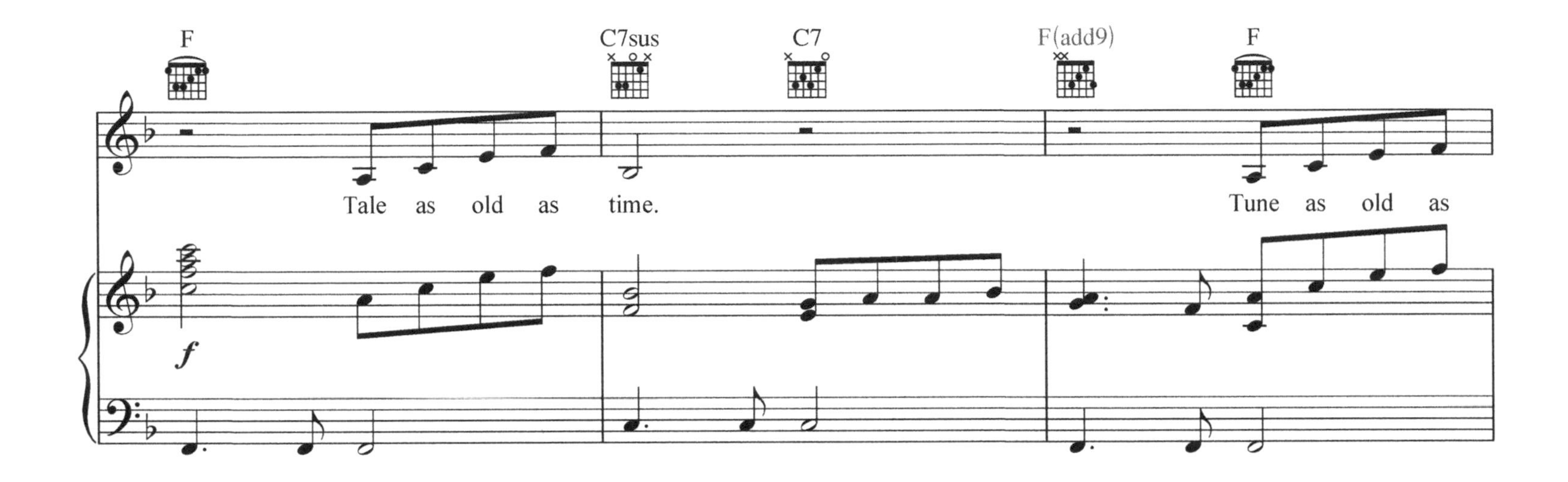
F
C7sus
C7
F(add9)
Tale as old as time. Tune as old as
f

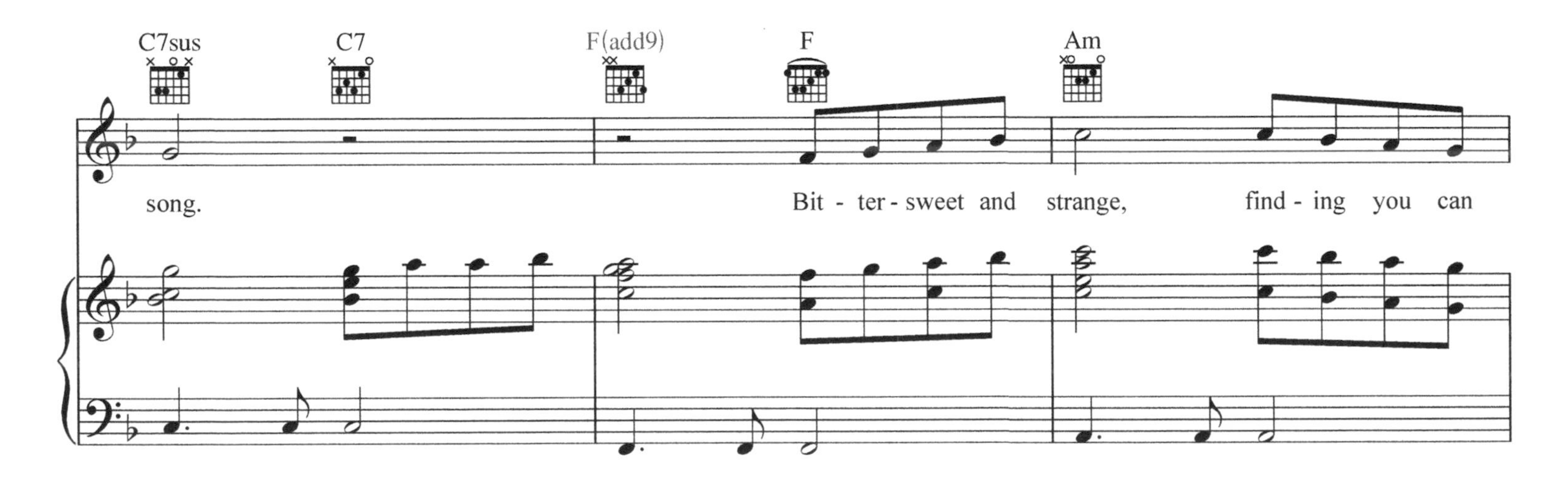
C7sus
C7
F(add9)
F
Am
song. Bit - ter - sweet and strange, find - ing you can

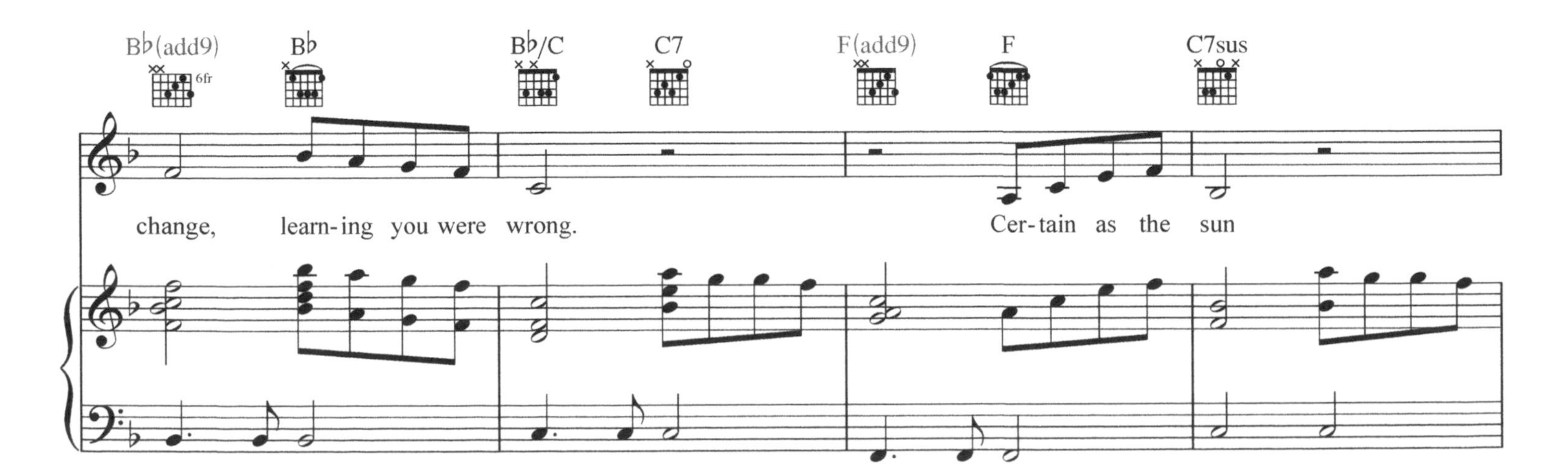
B♭(add9)
6fr
B♭
B♭/C
C7
F(add9)
F
C7sus
change, learn - ing you were wrong. Cer - tain as the sun

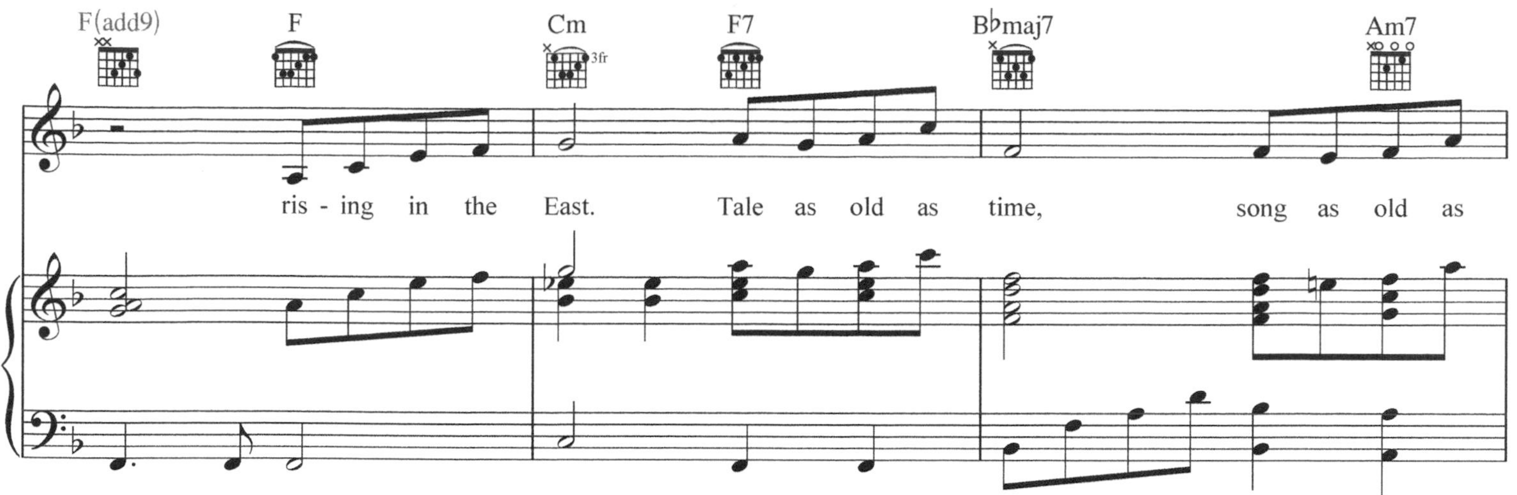
F(add9)
F
Cm
3fr
F7
B♭maj7
Am7
ris - ing in the East. Tale as old as time, song as old as

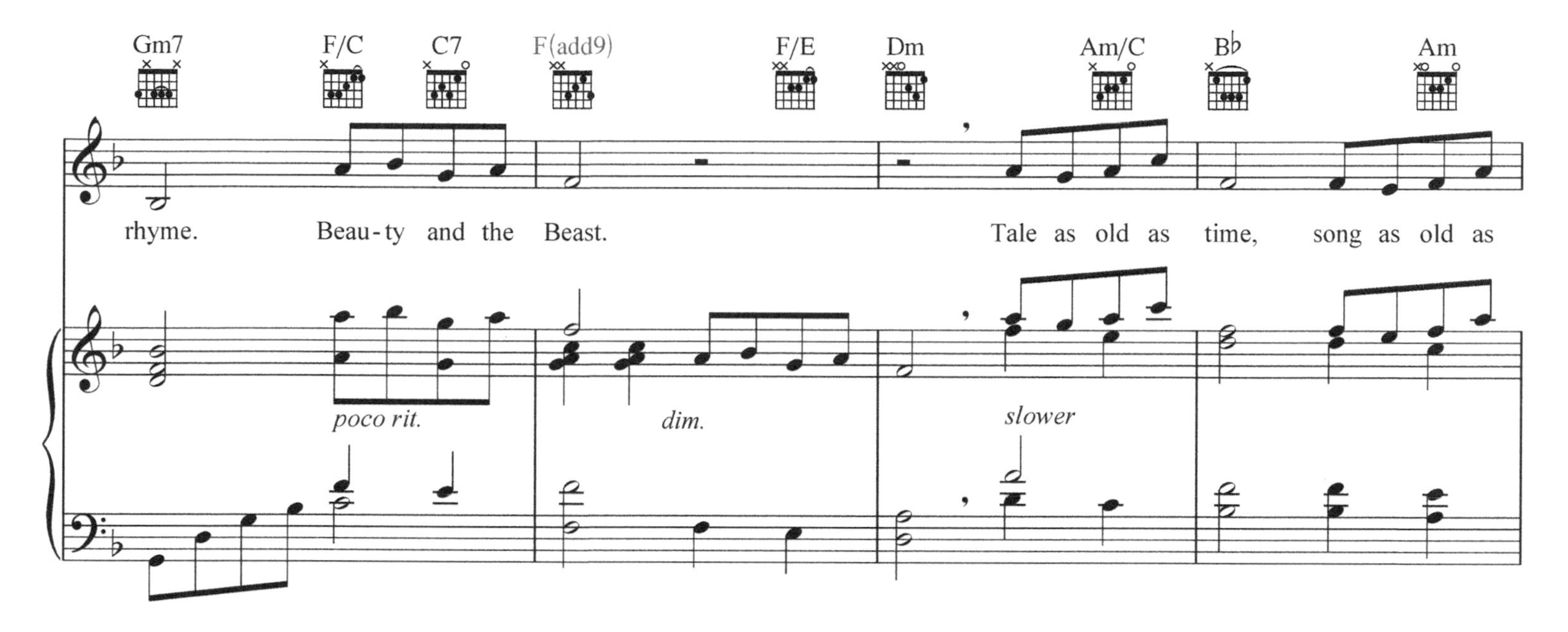
Gm7
F/C
C7
F(add9)
F/E
Dm
Am/C
B♭
Am
rhyme. Beau - ty and the Beast. Tale as old as time, song as old as
poco rit.
dim.
slower

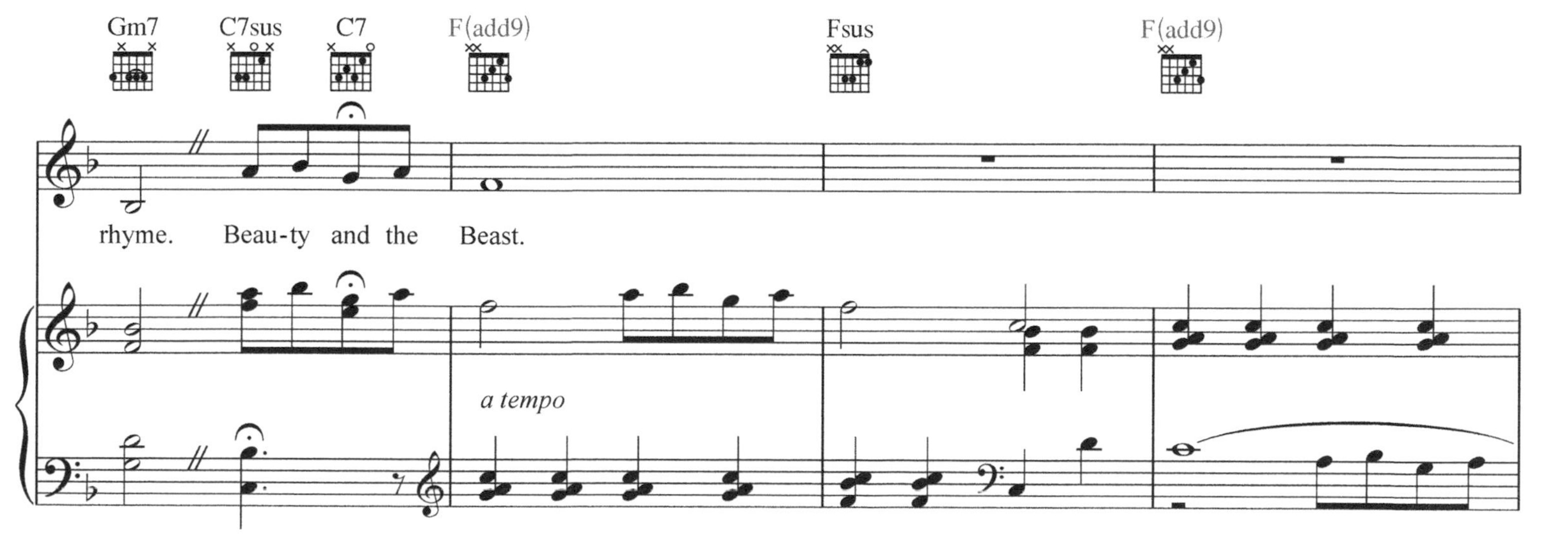
Gm7
C7sus
C7
F(add9)
Fsus
F(add9)
rhyme. Beau - ty and the Beast.
a tempo

Fsus
F
8va
rit.

CAN YOU FEEL THE LOVE TONIGHT

(Pop Version)

from Walt Disney Pictures' THE LION KING
as performed by Elton John

Music by ELTON JOHN
Lyrics by TIM RICE

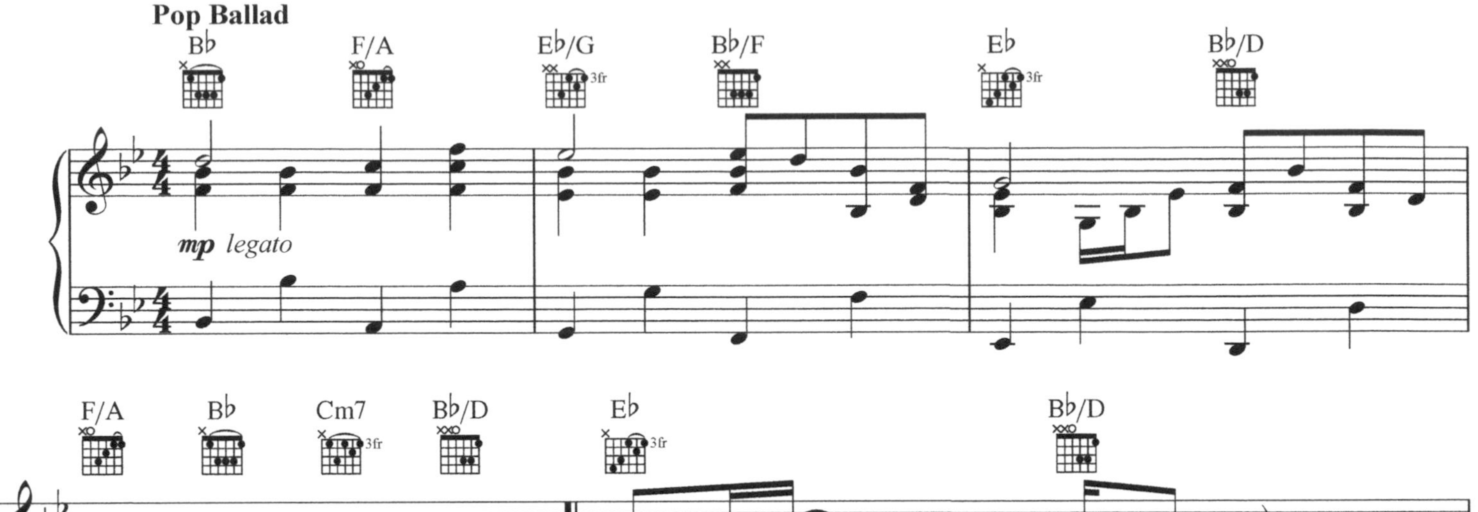

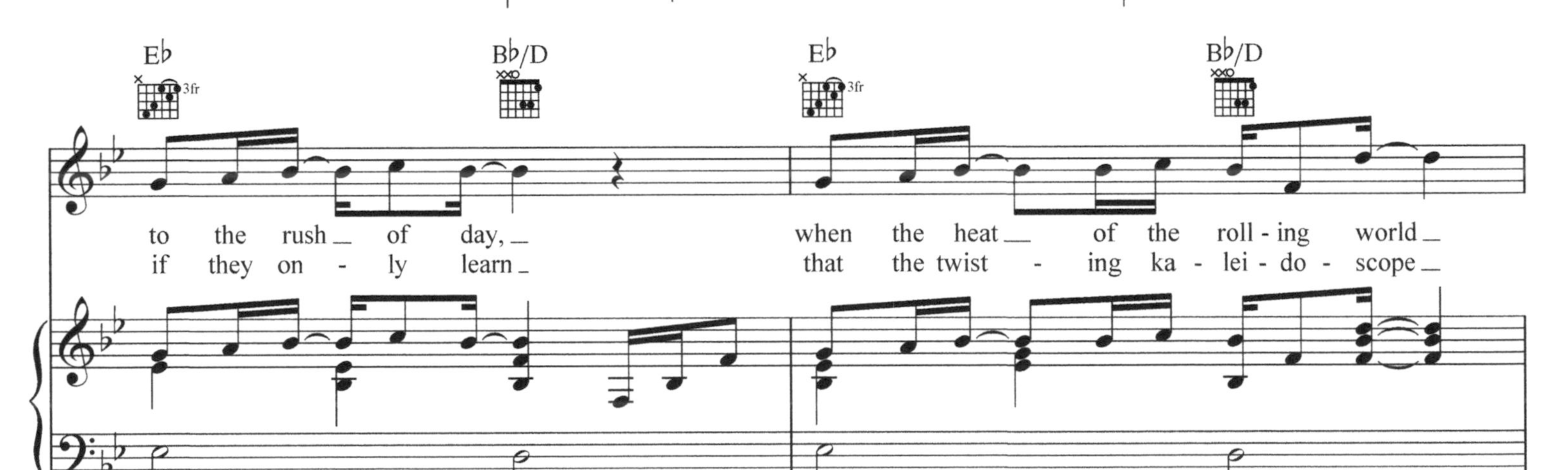

E♭
B♭/D
E♭
Gm
3fr
and it sees me through.
It's e-nough for this rest-less war-rior
to the wild out-doors
when the heart of this star-crossed voy-ag-er

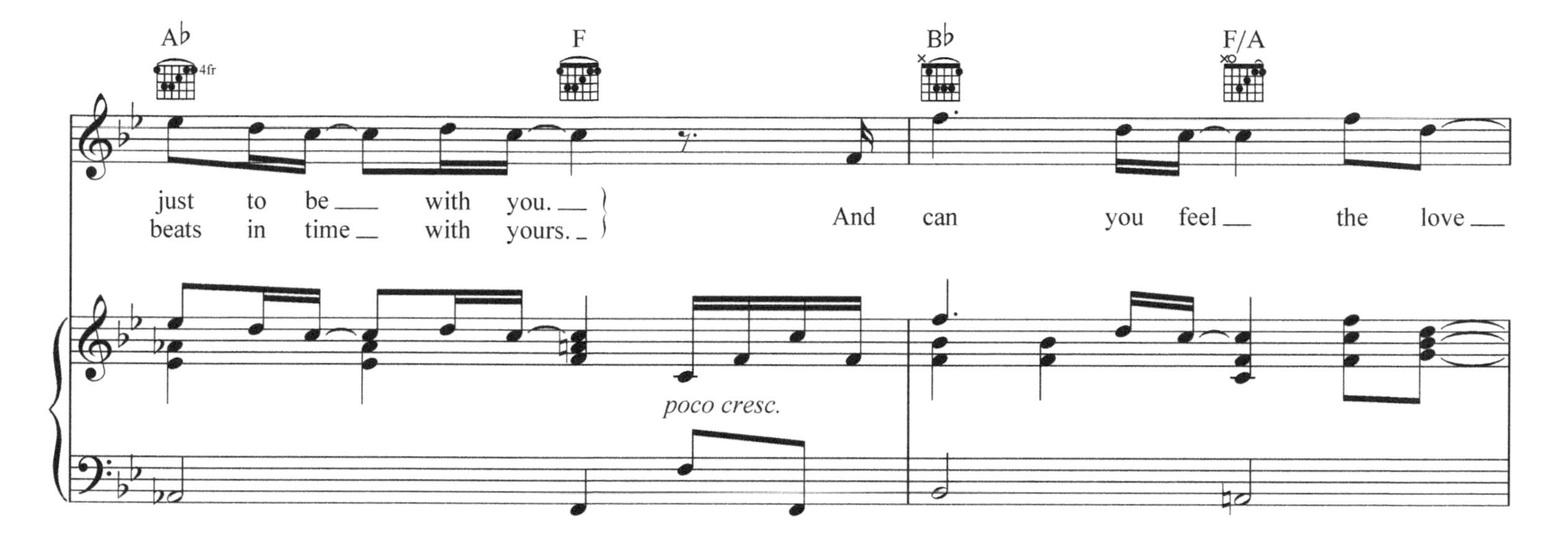
A♭
F
B♭
F/A
4fr
just to be with you.
beats in time with yours.
And can you feel the love
poco cresc.

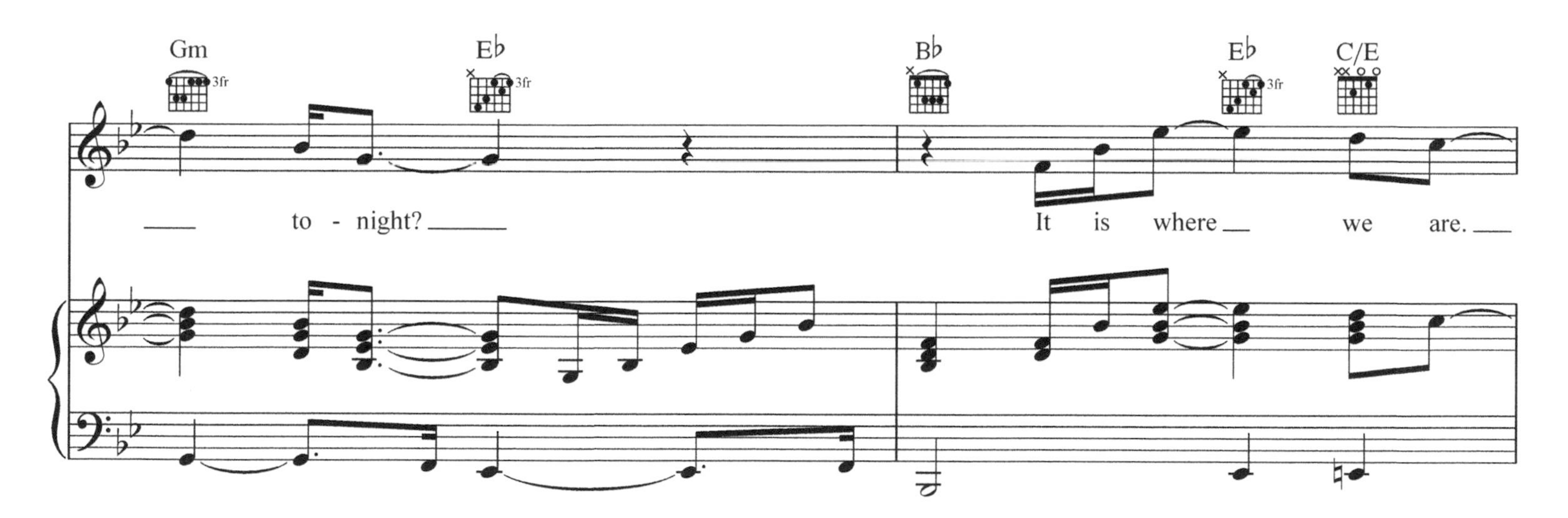
Gm
E♭
B♭
E♭
C/E
3fr
to-night?
It is where we are.

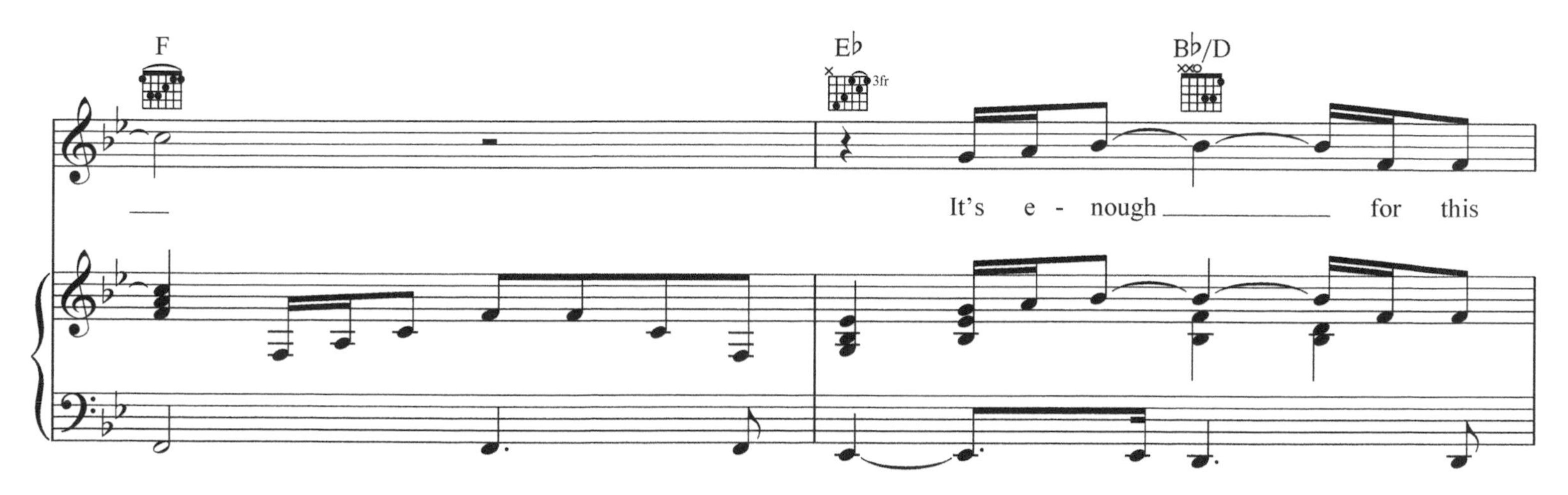
F
E♭
B♭/D
3fr
It's e-nough for this

Gm Gm/F E♭ Cm B♭/D E♭ C/E
3fr 3fr 3fr 3fr
wide - eyed wan - der - er that we got this far.

F B♭ F/A
And can you feel the love

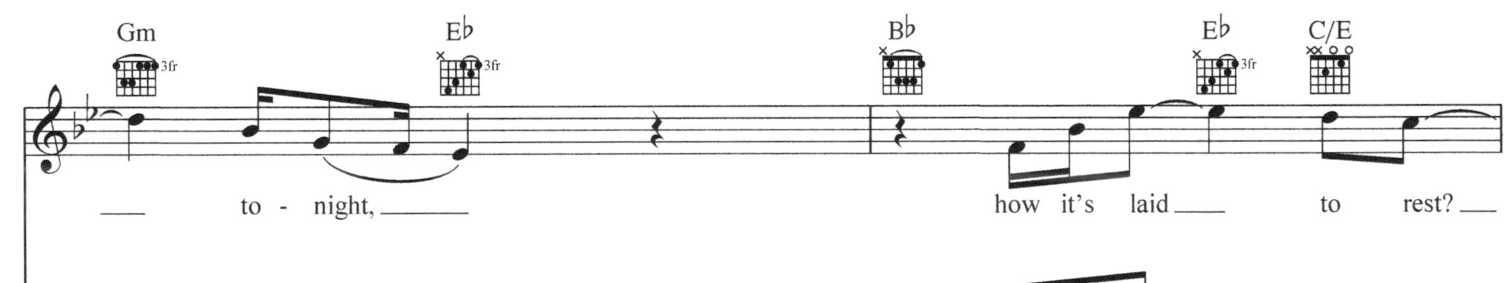
Gm E♭ B♭ E♭ C/E
3fr 3fr 3fr
to - night, how it's laid to rest?

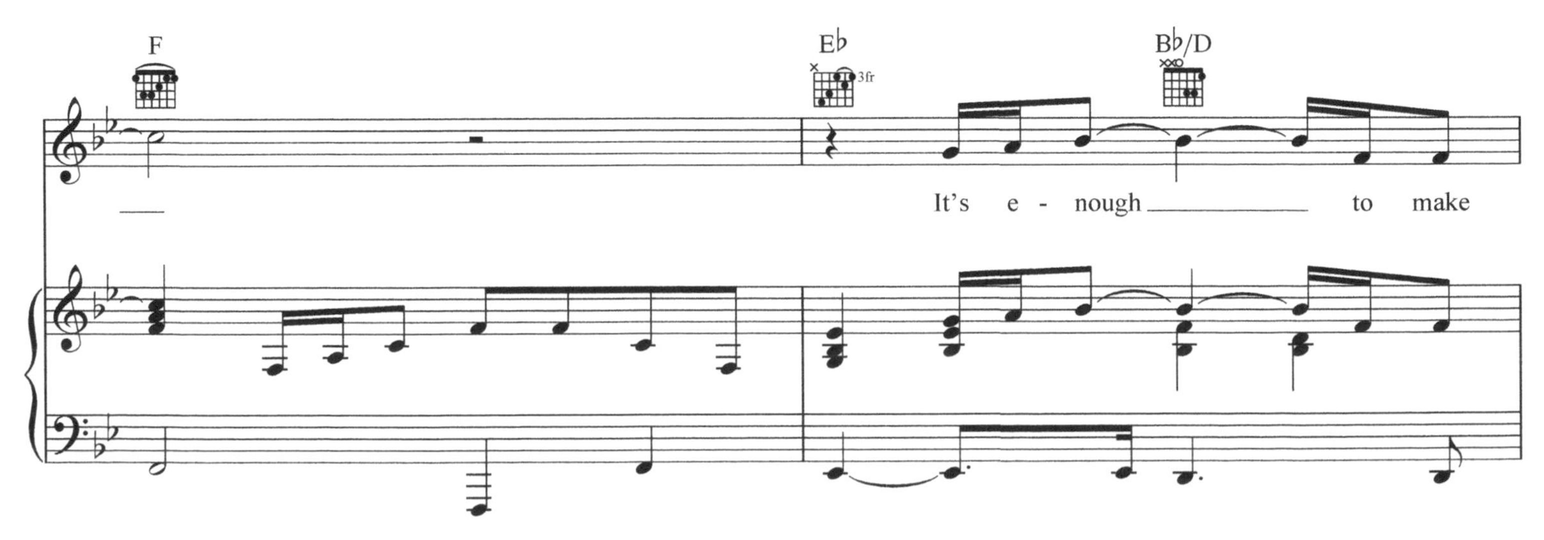
F E♭ B♭/D
3fr
It's e - nough to make

Gm
Gm/F
E♭
Cm
B♭/D
E♭
F7sus
kings and vag - a - bonds be - lieve the ver - y best.

E♭/B♭
B♭
1
F/A
E♭/G
B♭/F
poco dim.

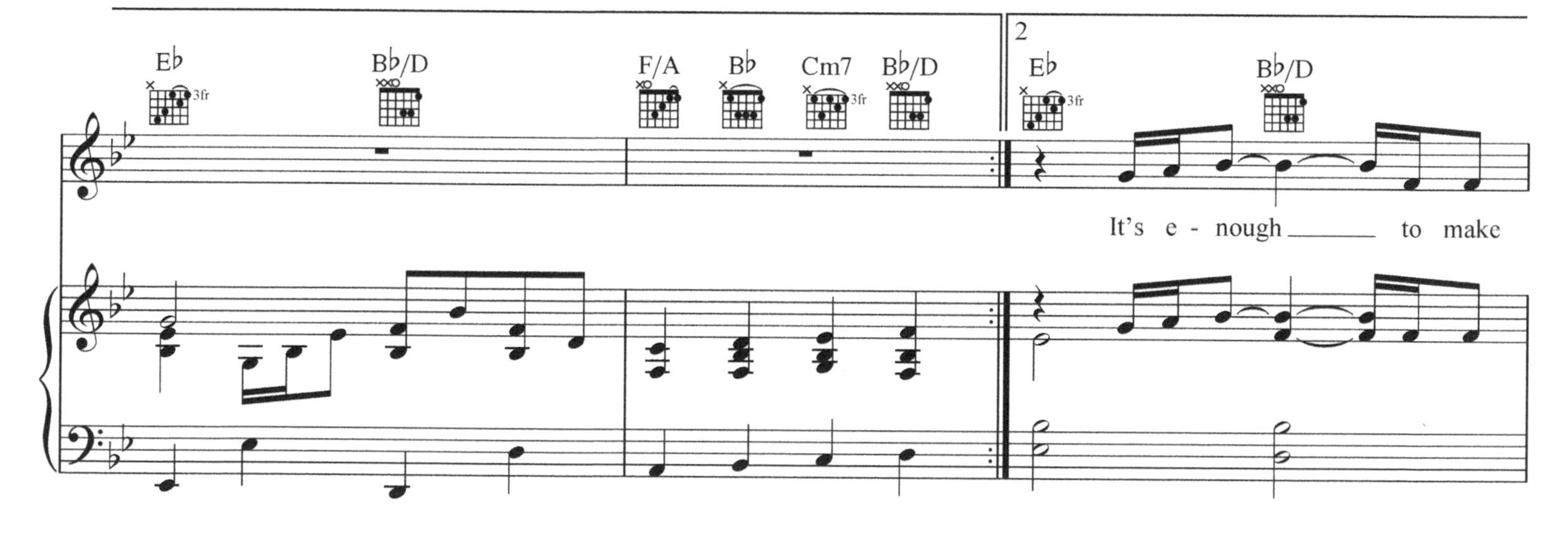
E♭
B♭/D
F/A
B♭
Cm7
B♭/D
2
E♭
B♭/D
It's e - nough to make

Gm
Gm/F
E♭
Cm
B♭/D
E♭
F7sus
E♭/B♭
B♭
kings and vag - a - bonds be - lieve the ver - y best.
molto rit.

COLORS OF THE WIND

(Pop Version)

from Walt Disney's POCAHONTAS
as performed by Vanessa Williams

Music by ALAN MENKEN
Lyrics by STEPHEN SCHWARTZ

Gm Dm E♭6 B♭/D
1
Cm F6
I know ev - 'ry rock and tree and crea - ture has a life, has a spir - it, has a
If you walk the foot-steps of a stran - ger, you'll learn
Gm F
2
Cm F E♭/F B♭ Dm/A
name. You things you nev - er knew you nev - er knew. Have you
Gm Dm E♭ Gm
ev - er heard the wolf cry to the blue corn moon or
asked the grin - ning bob - cat why he
let the ea - gle tell you where he's
Dm E♭ F/E♭ Dm7 Gm7
grinned?
been?
Can you sing with all the voic - es of the moun - tain? Can you

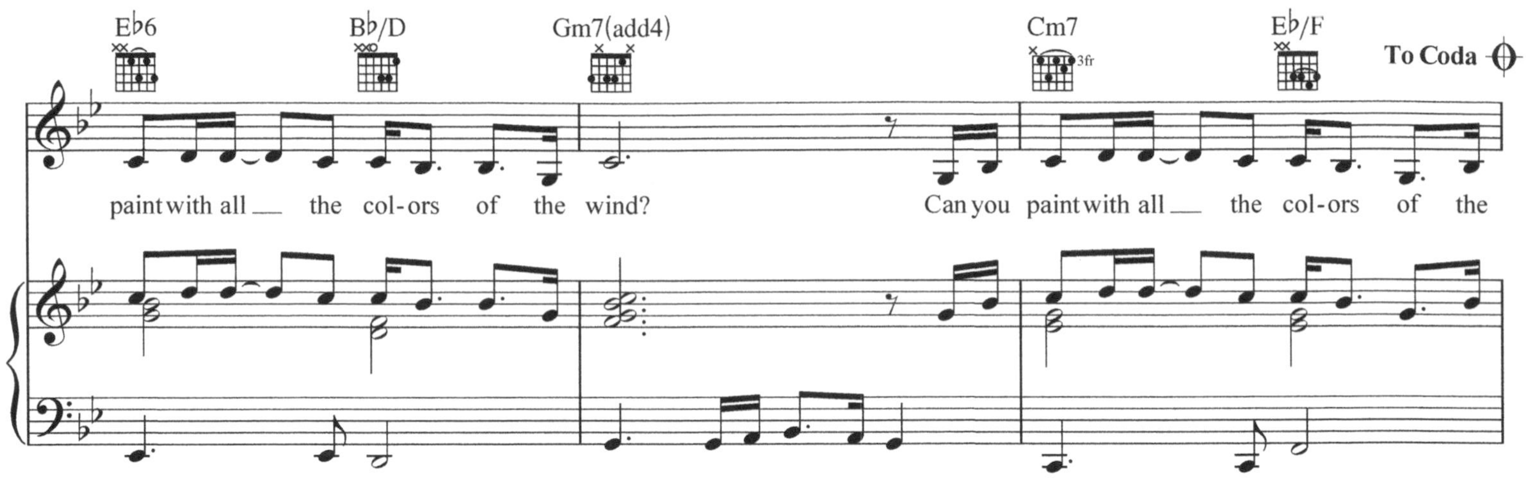
E♭6
B♭/D
Gm7(add4)
Cm7
3fr
E♭/F
To Coda
paint with all the col-ors of the wind?
Can you paint with all the col-ors of the

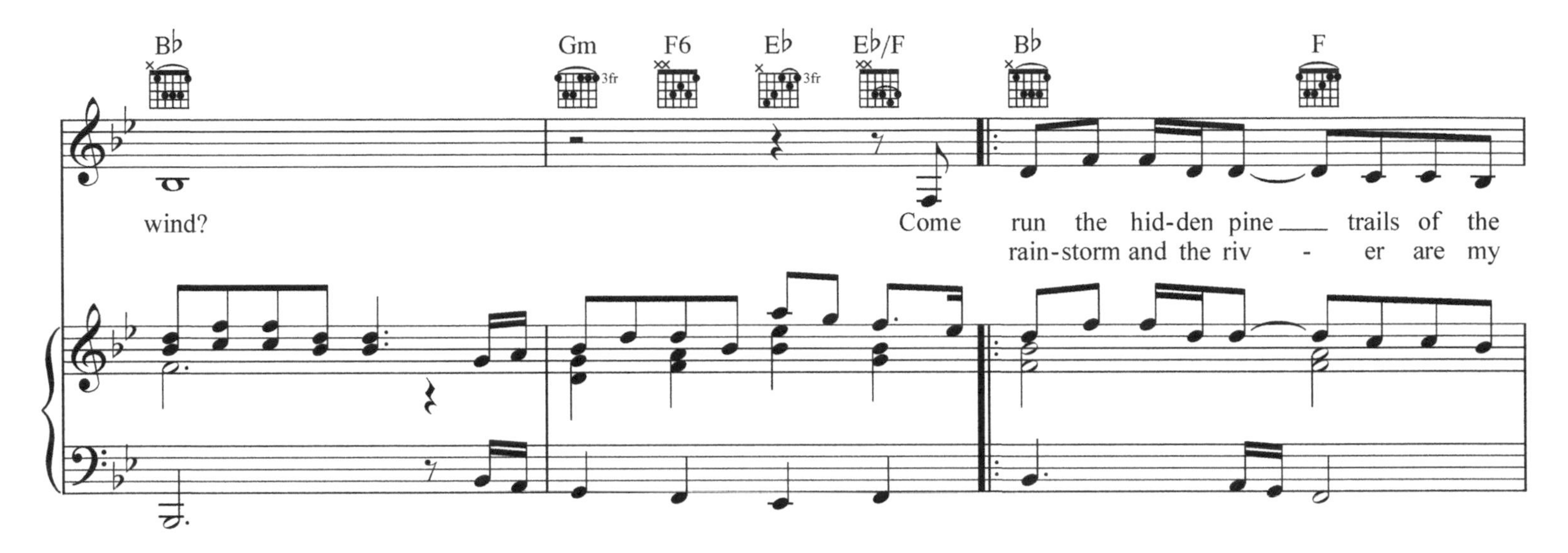
B♭
Gm
3fr
F6
E♭
3fr
E♭/F
B♭
F
wind?
Come run the hid-den pine trails of the
rain-storm and the riv - er are my

Gm
3fr
E♭(add9)
6fr
B♭
Dm7
for - est,
come taste the sun-sweet ber-ries of the earth,
come
broth-ers;
the her-on and the ot-ter are my friends;
and

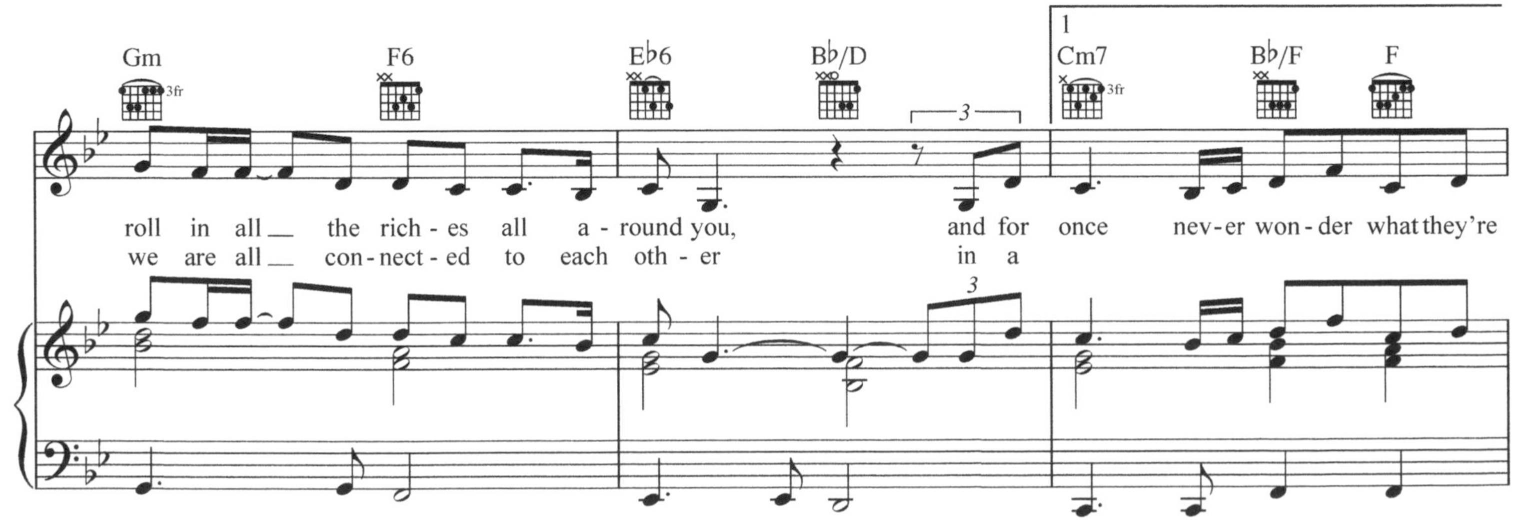
Gm
3fr
F6
E♭6
B♭/D
1
Cm7
3fr
B♭/F
F
3
roll in all the rich-es all a-round you,
and for once nev-er won-der what they're
we are all con-nect-ed to each oth-er
in a

D.S. al Coda
Gm
F(add9)/A
2
Cm7
E♭/F
B♭
Dm/A
3fr
worth. The cir - cle in a hoop that nev - er ends. Have you

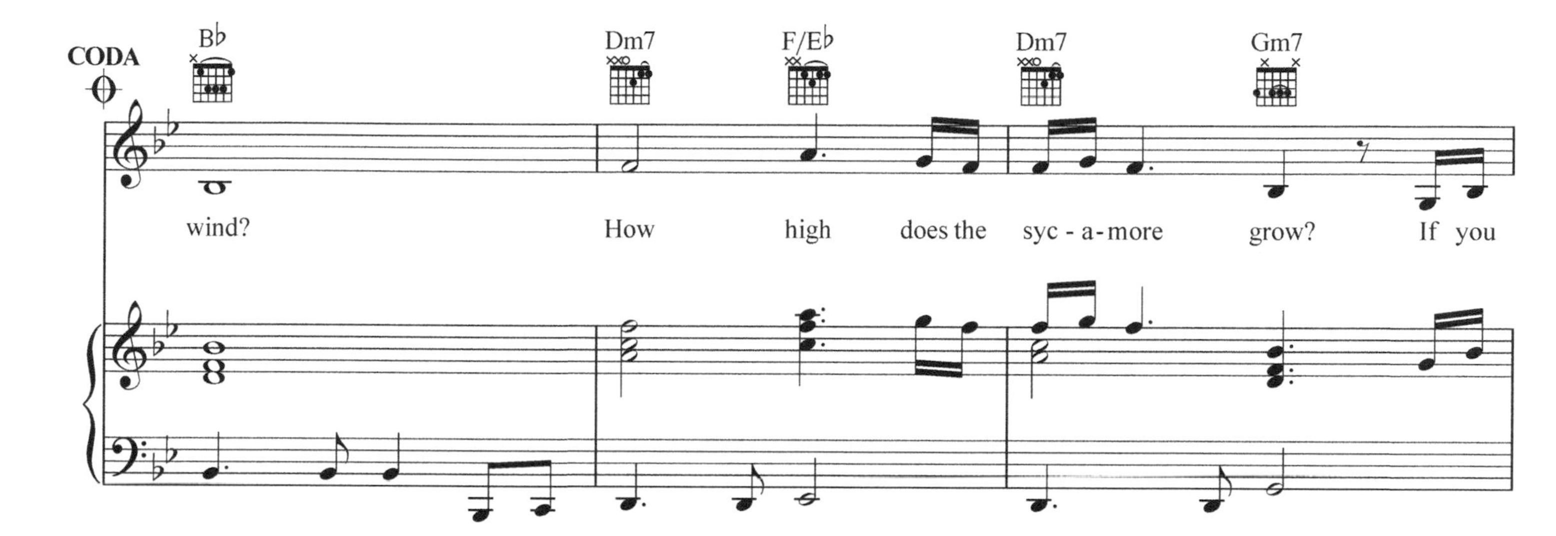
CODA
B♭
Dm7
F/E♭
Dm7
Gm7
wind? How high does the syc - a - more grow? If you

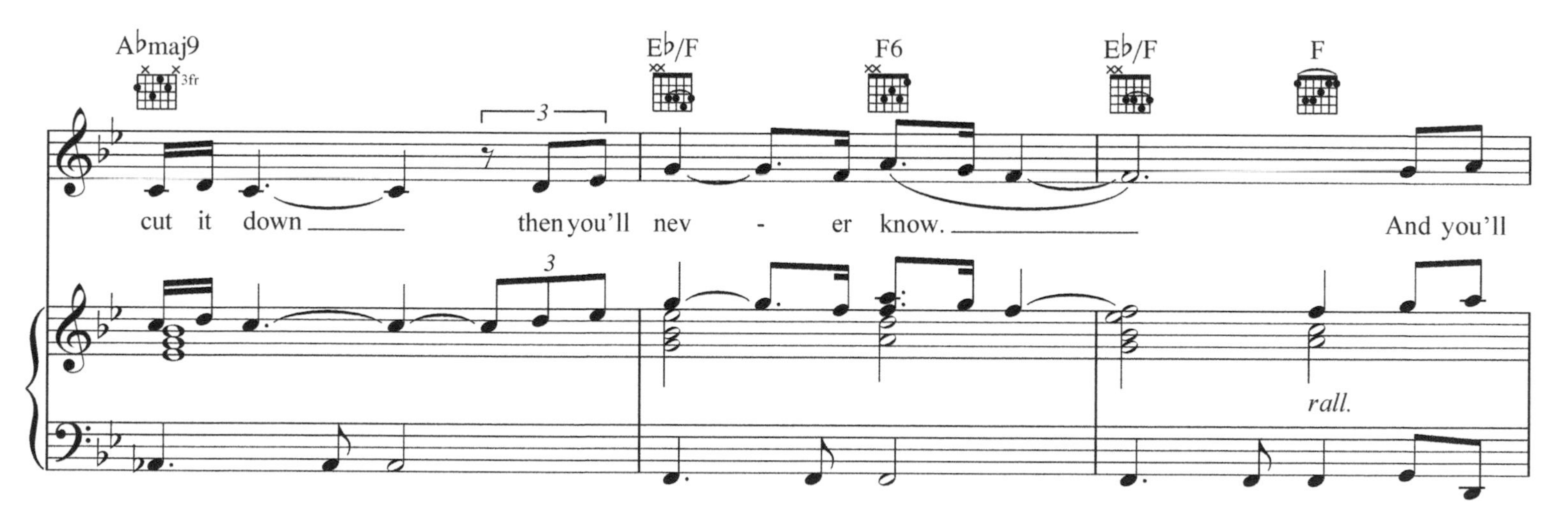
A♭maj9
E♭/F
F6
E♭/F
F
3fr
3
cut it down then you'll nev - er know. And you'll
rall.

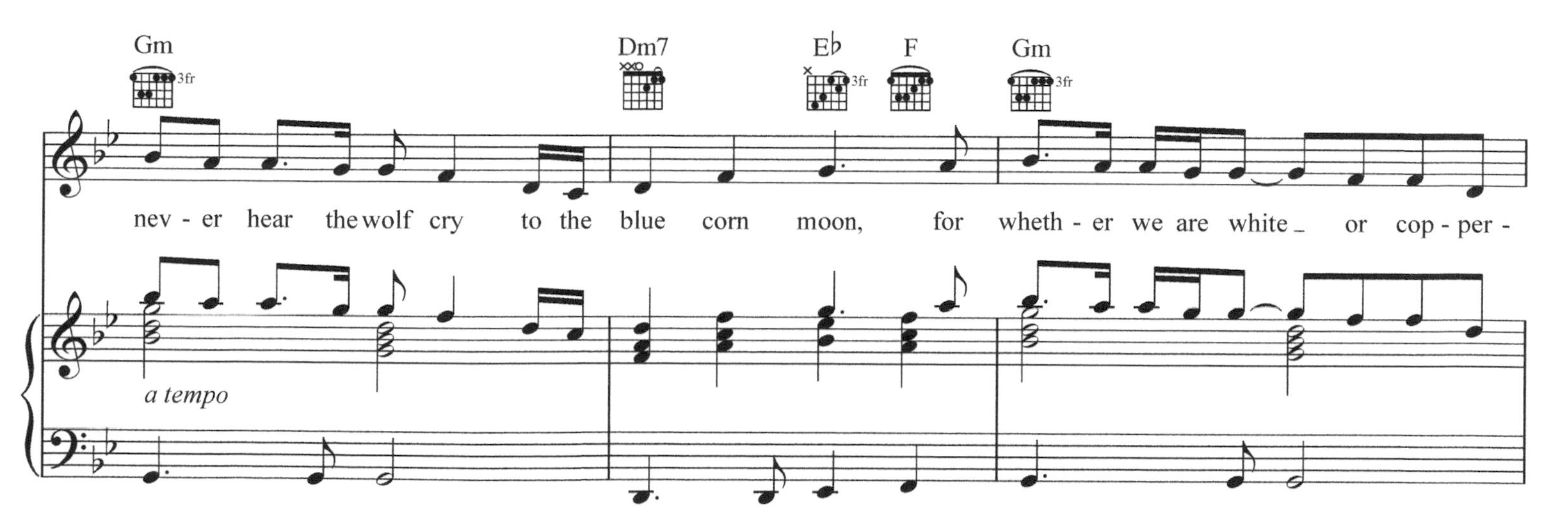
Gm
Dm7
E♭
F
Gm
3fr
nev - er hear the wolf cry to the blue corn moon, for wheth - er we are white or cop - per -
a tempo

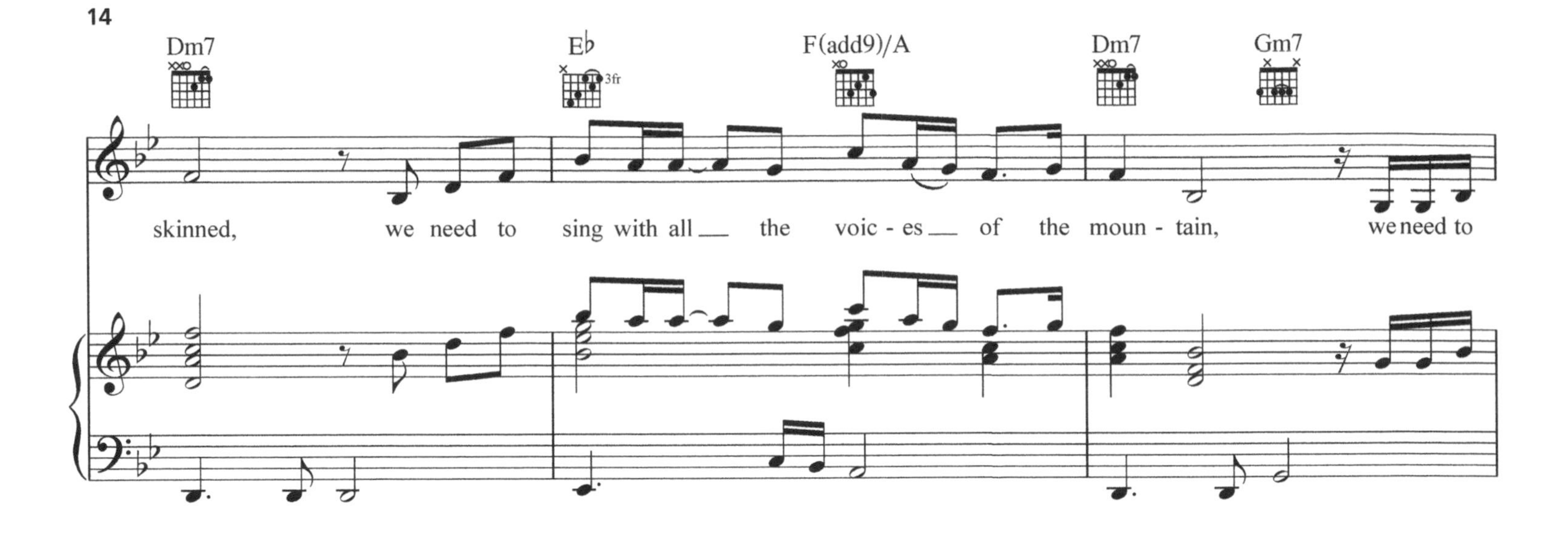
Dm7
E♭
3fr
F(add9)/A
Dm7
Gm7
skinned, we need to sing with all __ the voic - es __ of the moun - tain, we need to

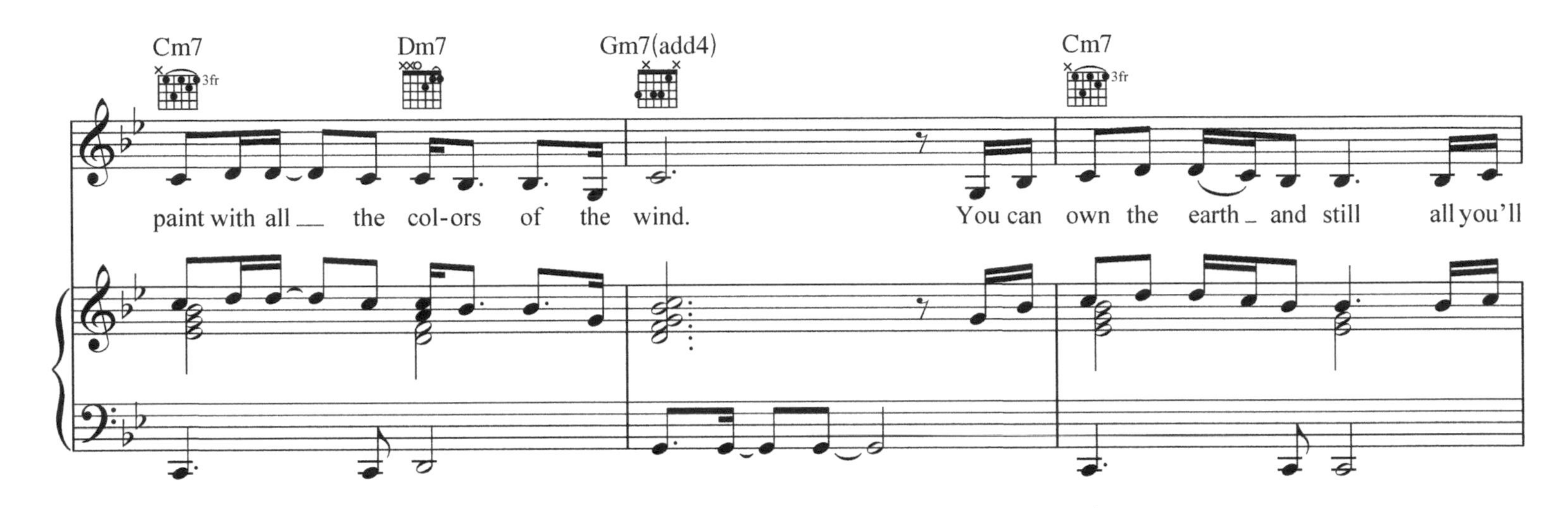
Cm7
3fr
Dm7
Gm7(add4)
Cm7
3fr
paint with all __ the col-ors of the wind. You can own the earth _ and still all you'll

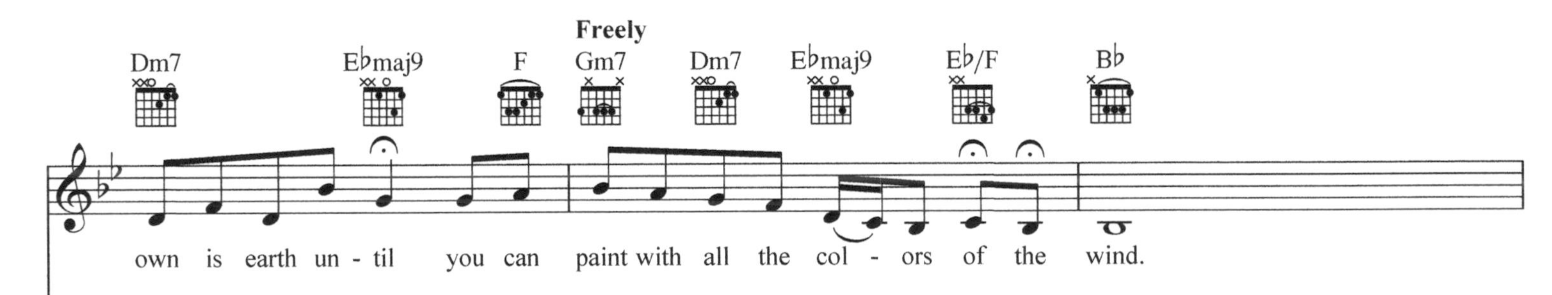
Freely
Dm7
E♭maj9
F
Gm7
Dm7
E♭maj9
E♭/F
B♭
own is earth un - til you can paint with all the col - ors of the wind.

a tempo

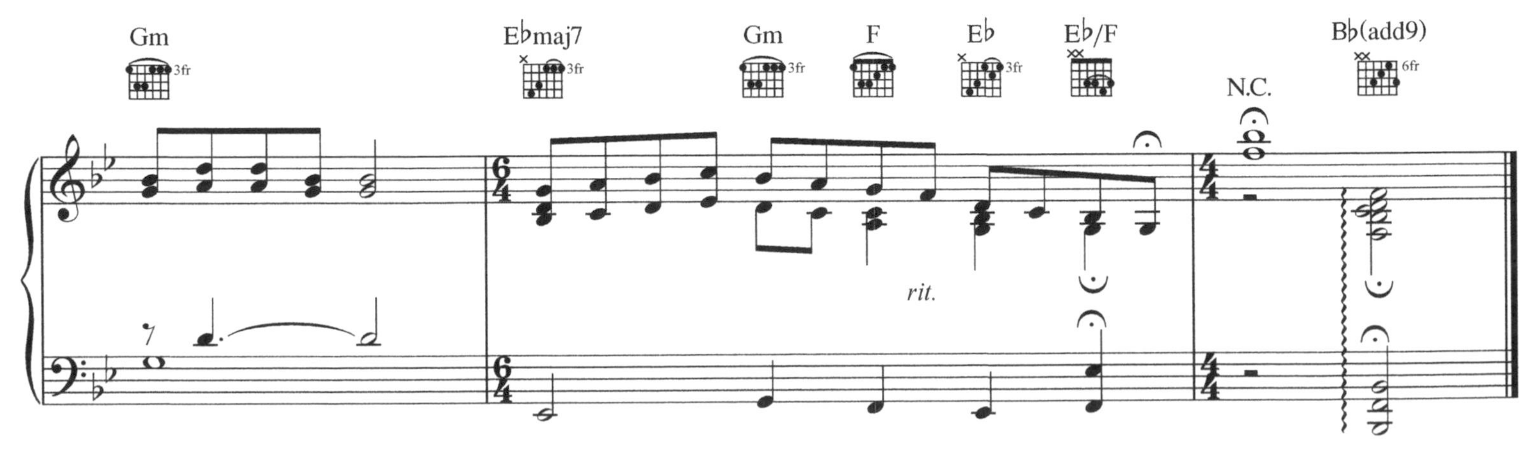
Gm
3fr
E♭maj7
3fr
Gm
3fr
F
E♭
3fr
E♭/F
N.C.
B♭(add9)
6fr
rit.

GO THE DISTANCE

from Walt Disney Pictures' HERCULES
as performed by Michael Bolton

Music by ALAN MENKEN
Lyrics by DAVID ZIPPEL

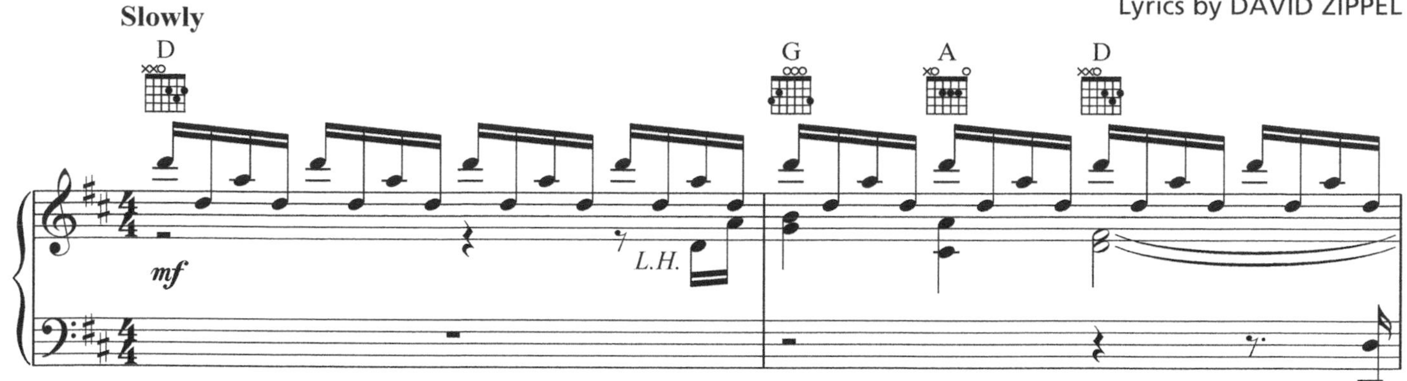

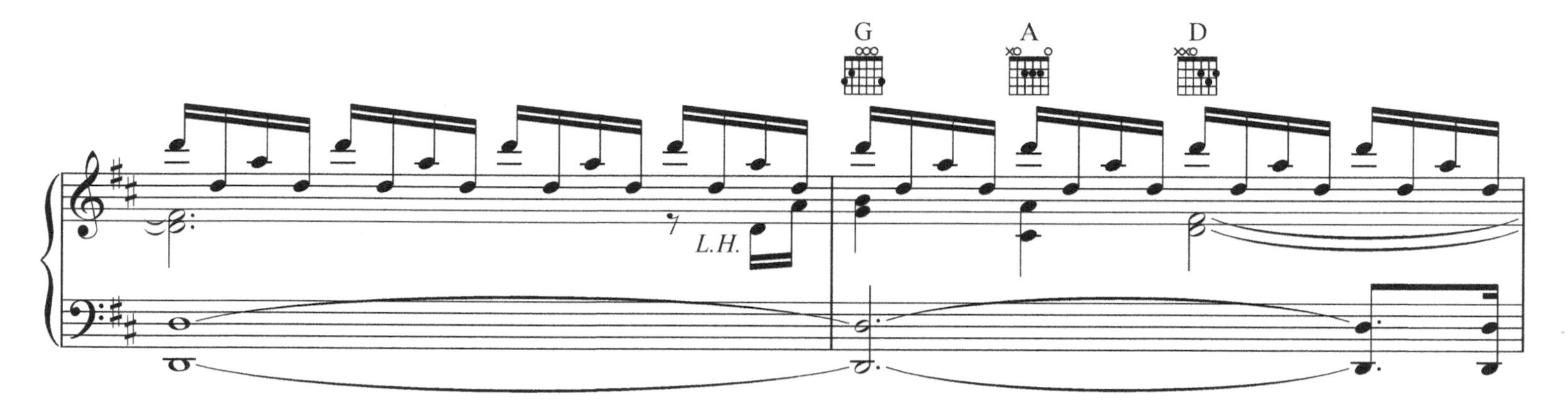

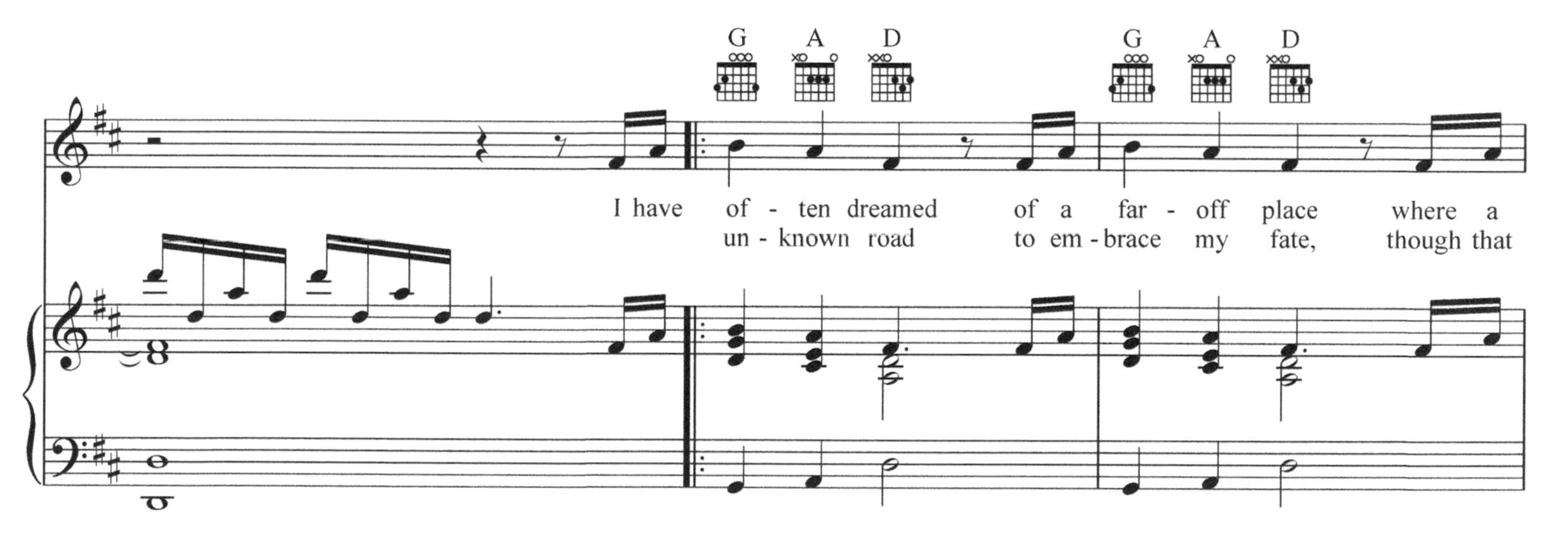

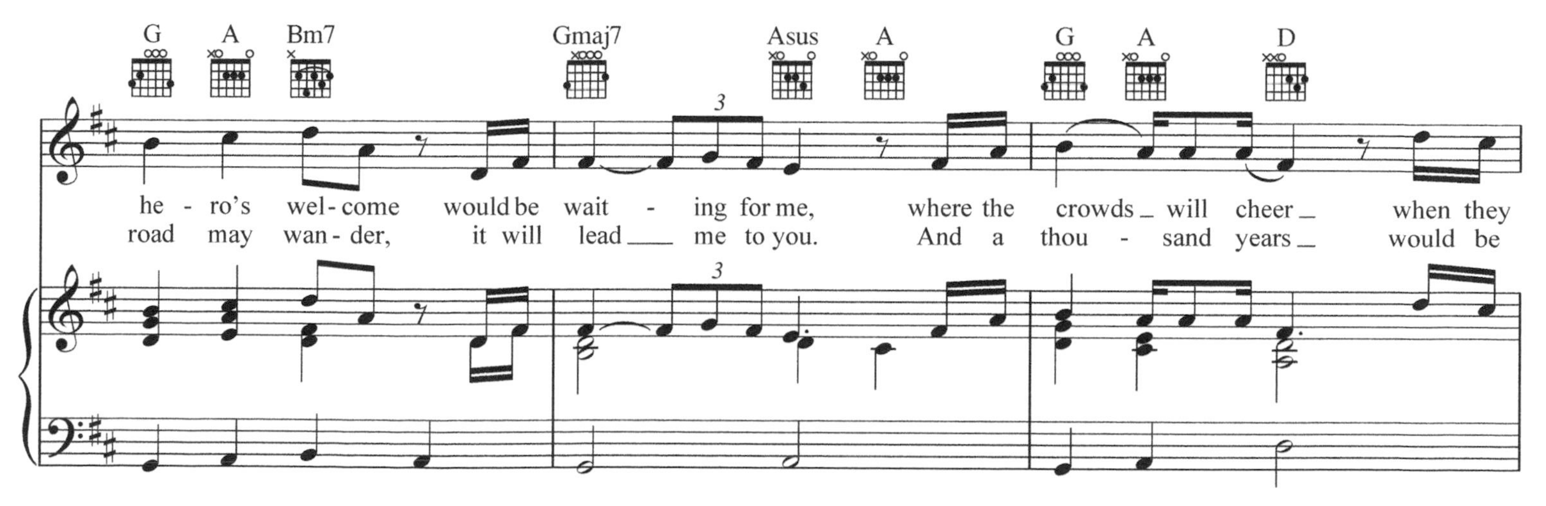

G A Bm G F♯ Bm D/A G Asus A
see my face, and a voice keeps say - ing this is where I'm meant to be. I'll be
worth the wait. It might take a life - time, but some - how I'll see it through. And I

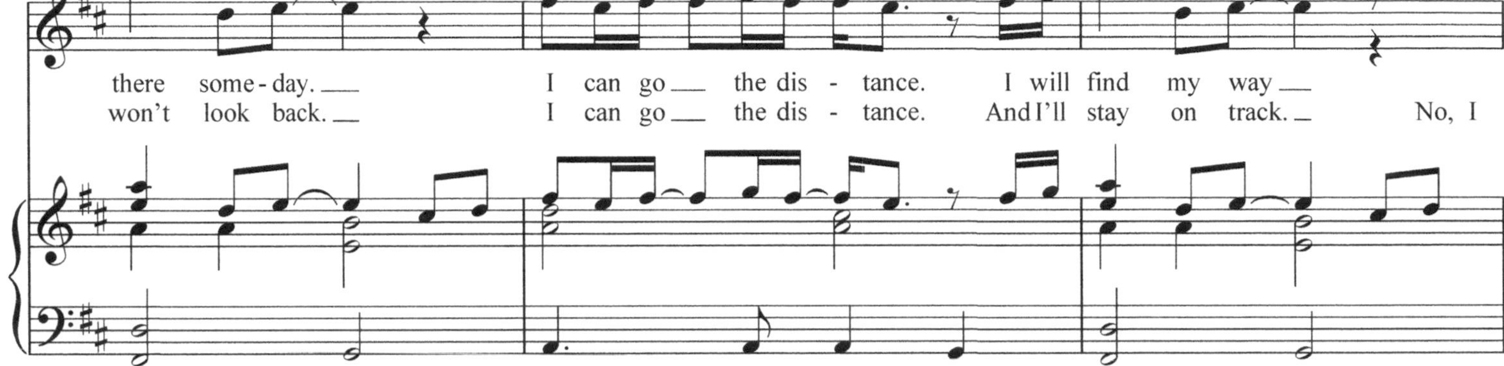
D(add9)/F♯ Em/G D/A A A/G D(add9)/F♯ Em/G
there some - day. I can go the dis - tance. I will find my way
won't look back. I can go the dis - tance. And I'll stay on track. No, I

D/A A A/G D(add9)/F♯ G 1 Bm7
if I can be strong. I know ev - 'ry mile will be worth my while.
won't ac - cept de - feat. It's an up - hill slope, but I

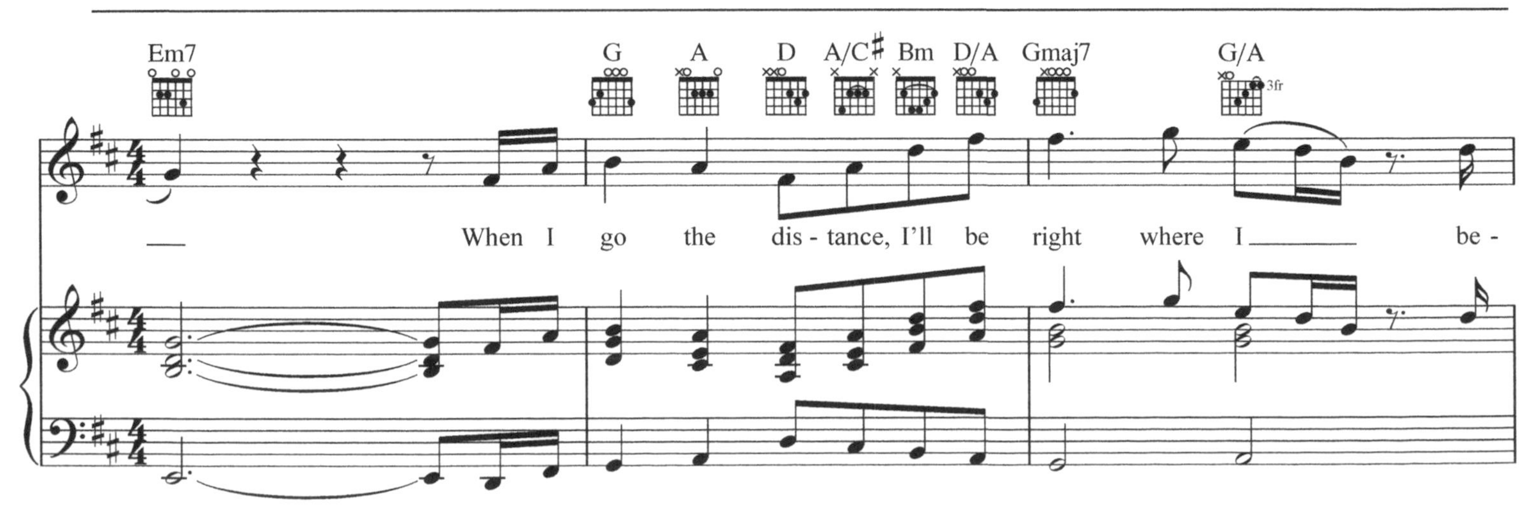
Em7 G A D A/C♯ Bm D/A Gmaj7 G/A
3fr
When I go the dis - tance, I'll be right where I be -

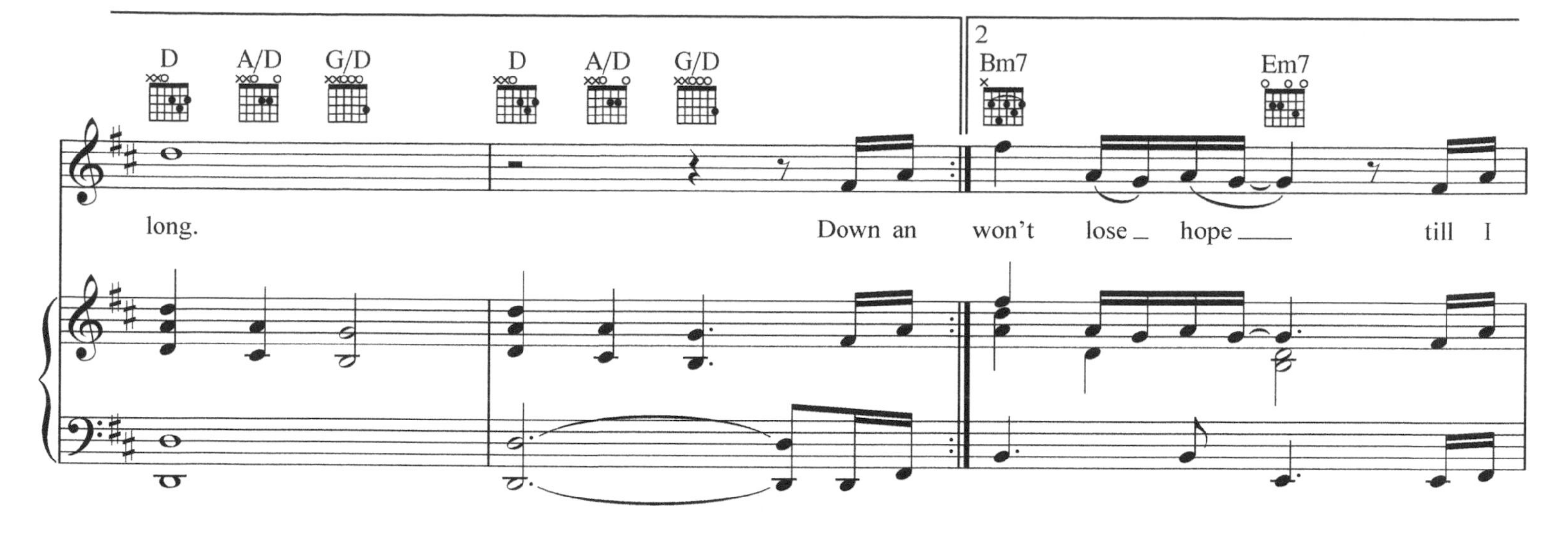
2
D A/D G/D D A/D G/D Bm7 Em7
long. Down an won't lose hope till I

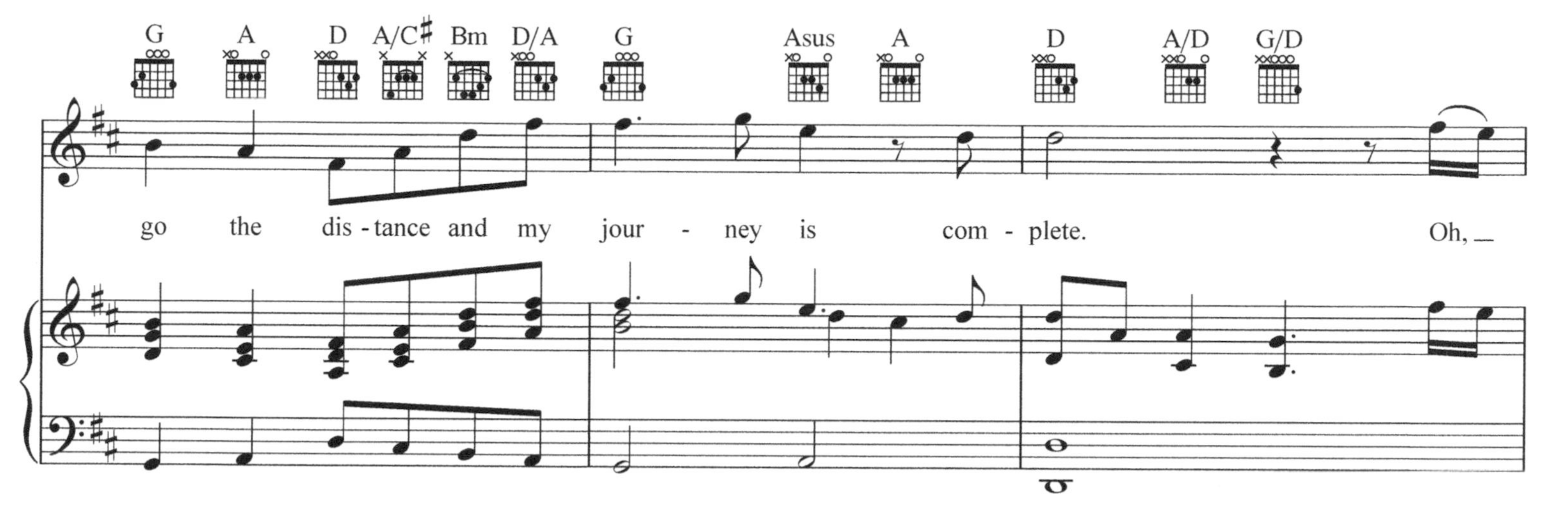
G A D A/C♯ Bm D/A G Asus A D A/D G/D
go the dis-tance and my jour - ney is com - plete. Oh,

D A/D G/D F B♭/D C/E A/C♯
yeah. But to look be - yond the glo - ry is the hard - est part, for a

D G F♯/A♯ E/G♯ F♯/A♯ B
he-ro's strength is meas - ured by his heart.

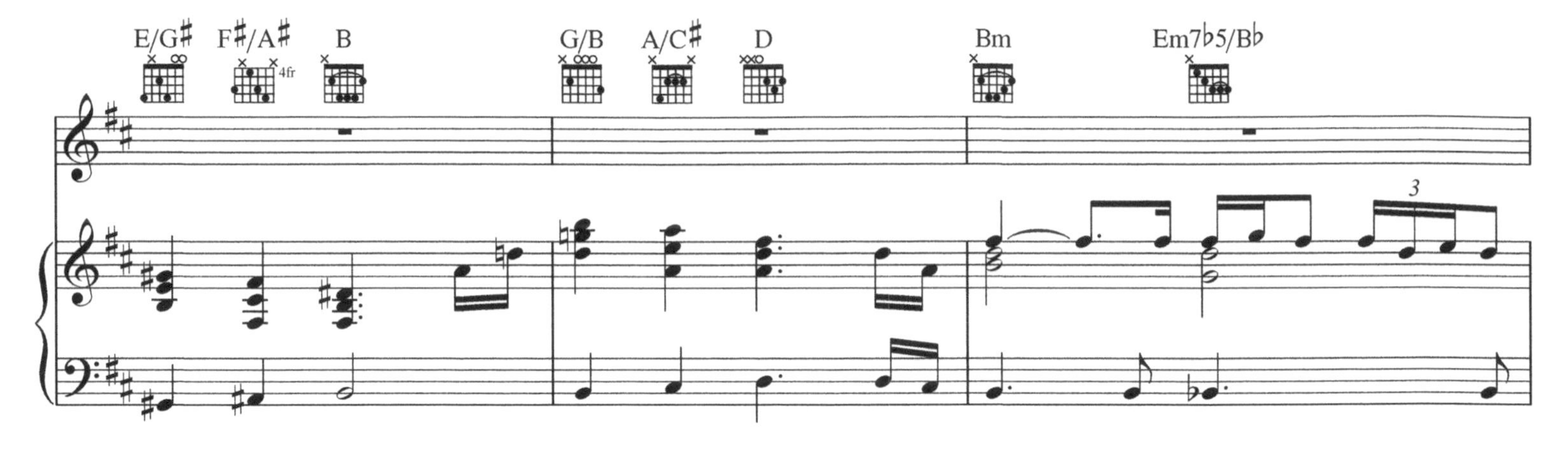
E/G♯
F♯/A♯
B
G/B
A/C♯
D
Bm
Em7♭5/B♭

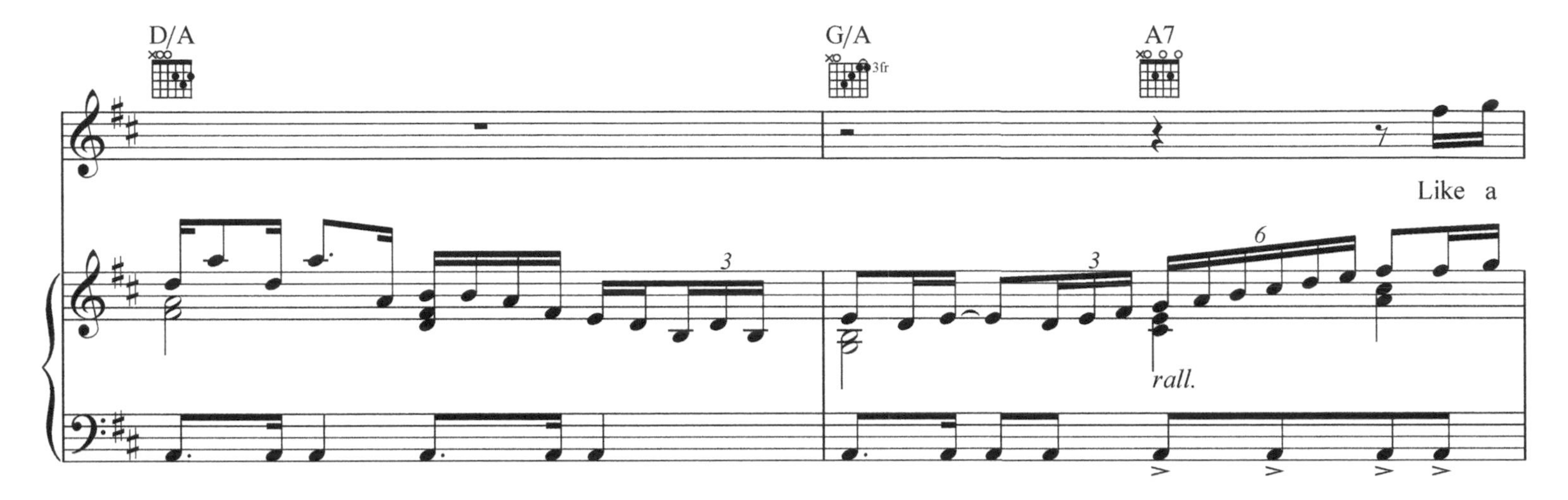
D/A
G/A
A7
Like a
rall.

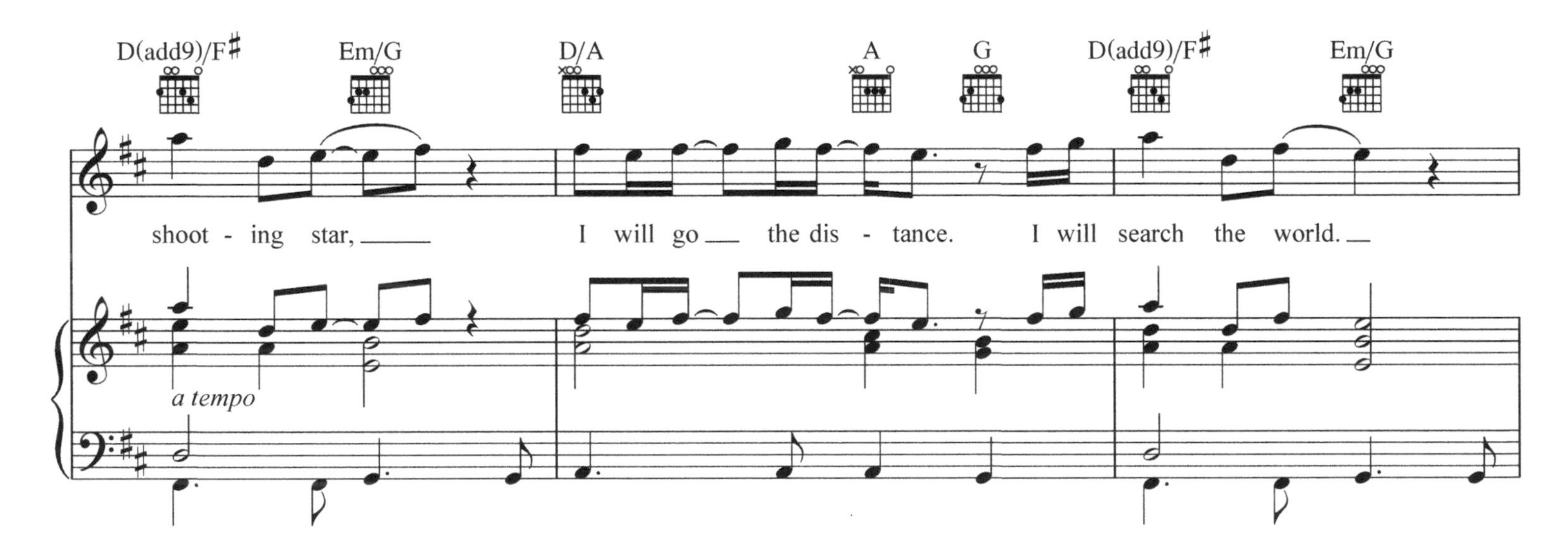
D(add9)/F♯
Em/G
D/A
A
G
D(add9)/F♯
Em/G
shoot - ing star,
I will go the dis - tance.
I will search the world.
a tempo

D/A
A
G
D(add9)/F♯
E/G♯
F♯/A♯
Bm
I will face its harms.
I don't care how far.
I can go the dis - tance till I

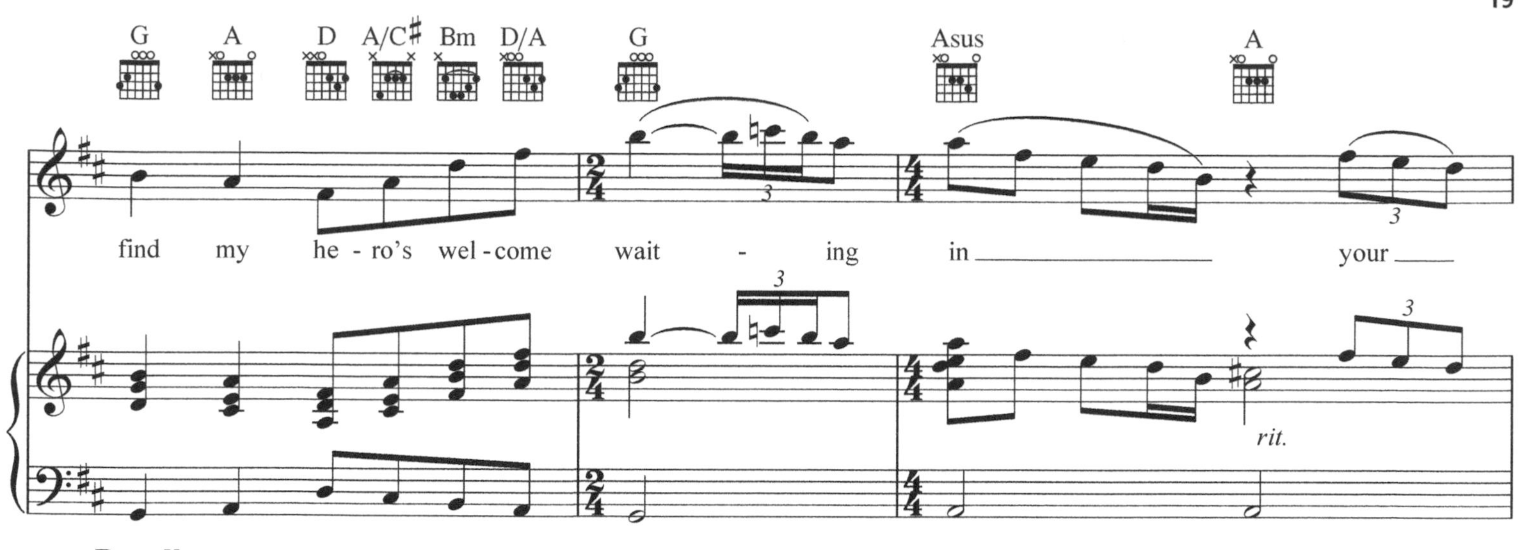
G
A
D
A/C♯
Bm
D/A
G
Asus
A
find my he - ro's wel - come wait - ing in your
rit.

Broadly
D5
5fr
Asus
arms.
I will

D(add9)/F♯
Gmaj7
Bm7
Em11
5fr
search the world. I will face its harms till I

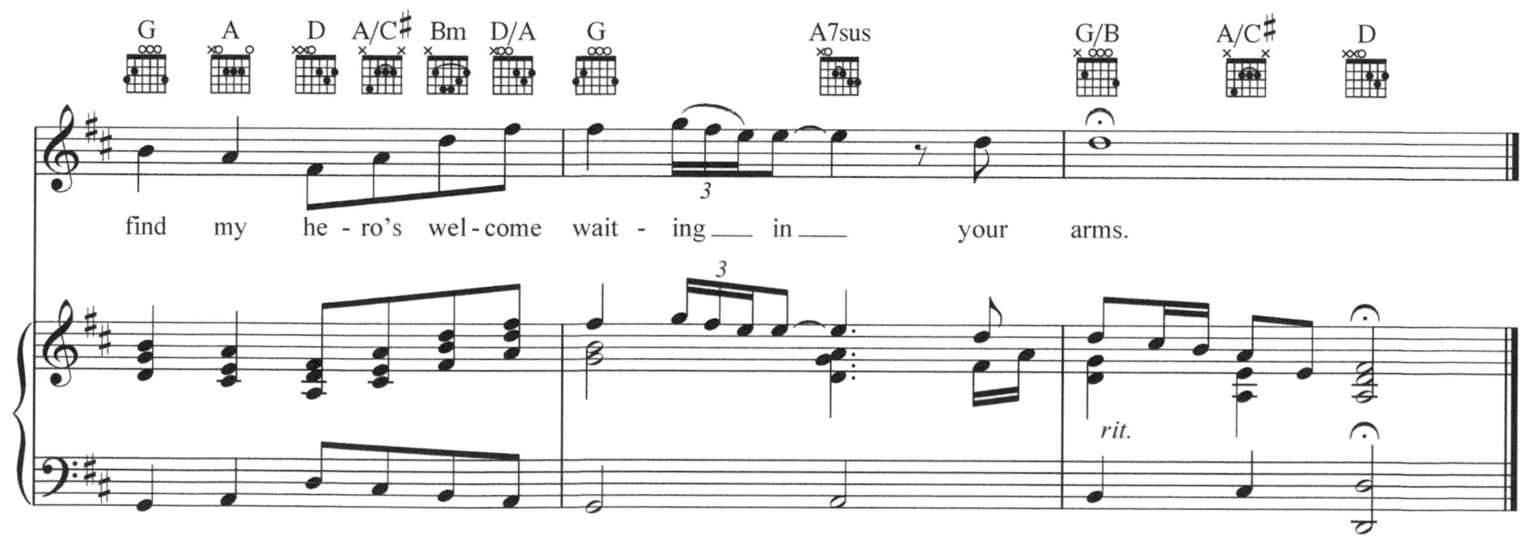
G
A
D
A/C♯
Bm
D/A
G
A7sus
G/B
A/C♯
D
find my he - ro's wel - come wait - ing in your arms.
rit.

LOOK THROUGH MY EYES

from Walt Disney Pictures' BROTHER BEAR

Words and Music by
PHIL COLLINS

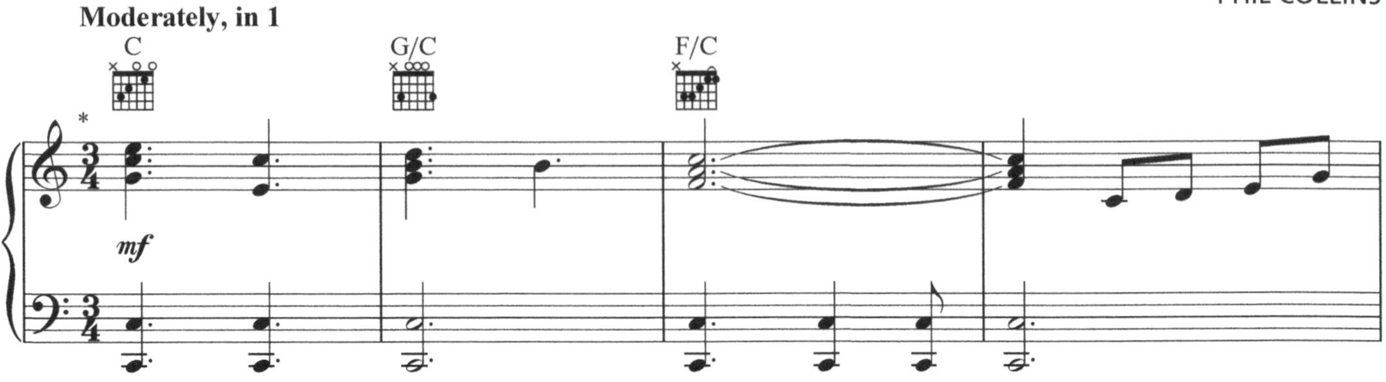

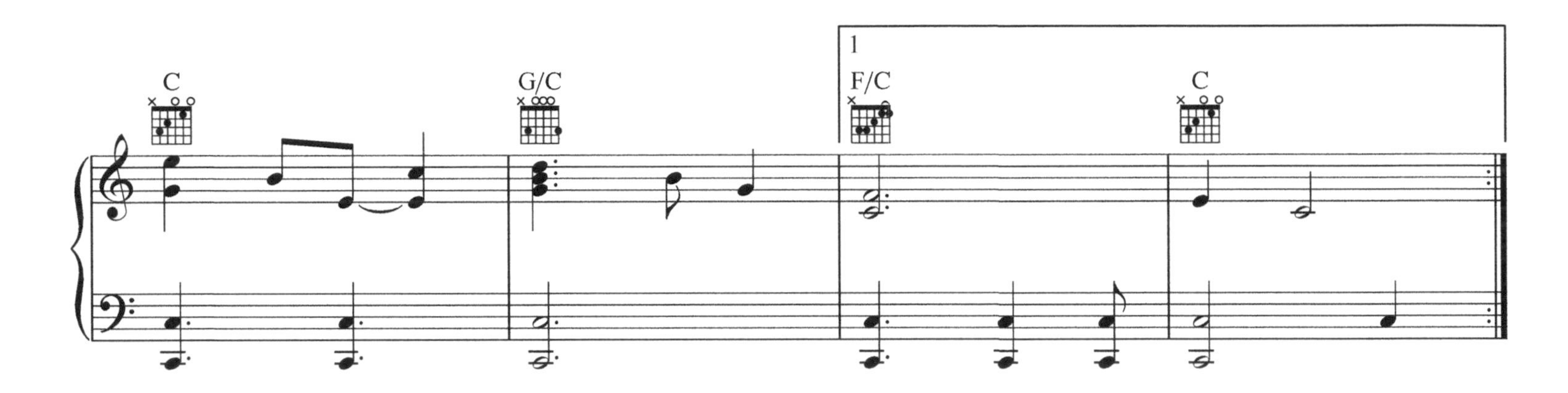

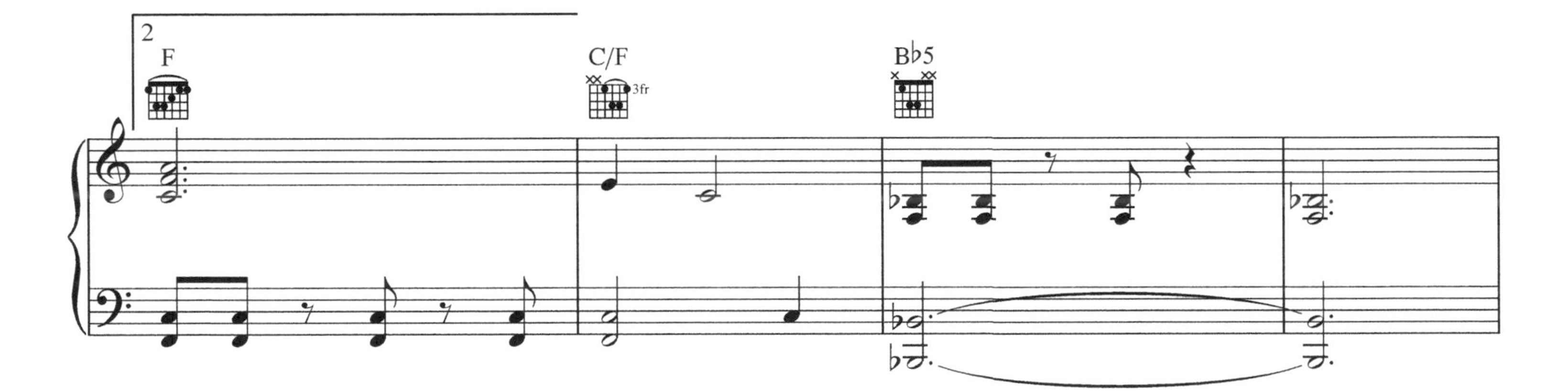

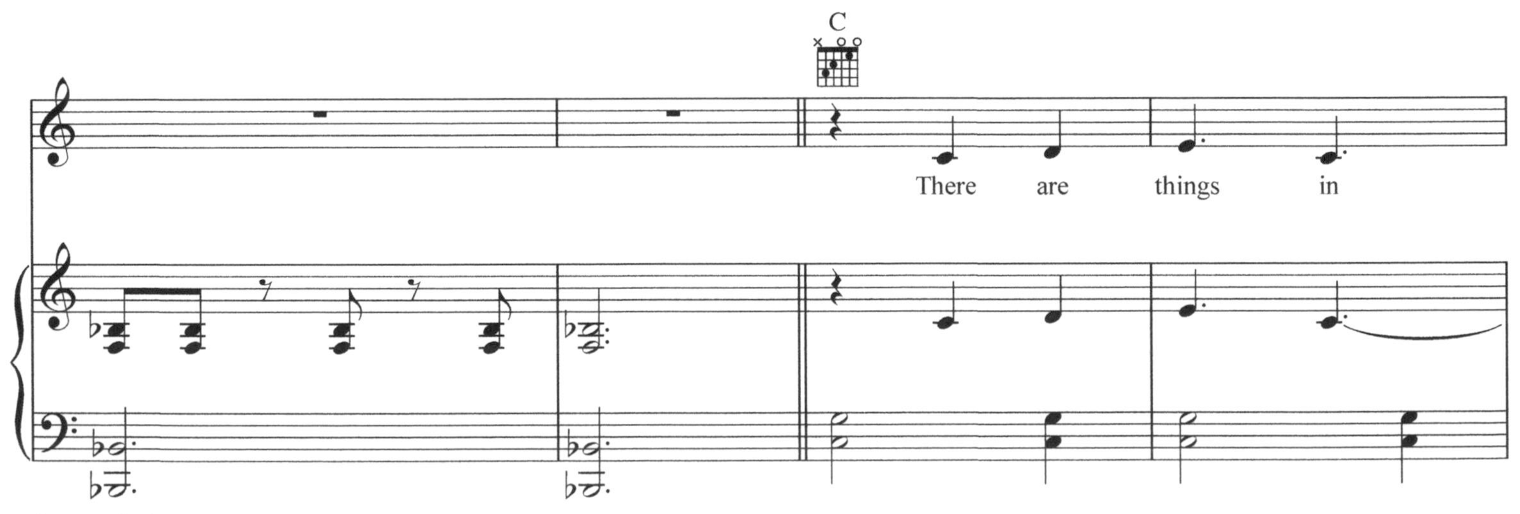

*Recorded a whole step higher.

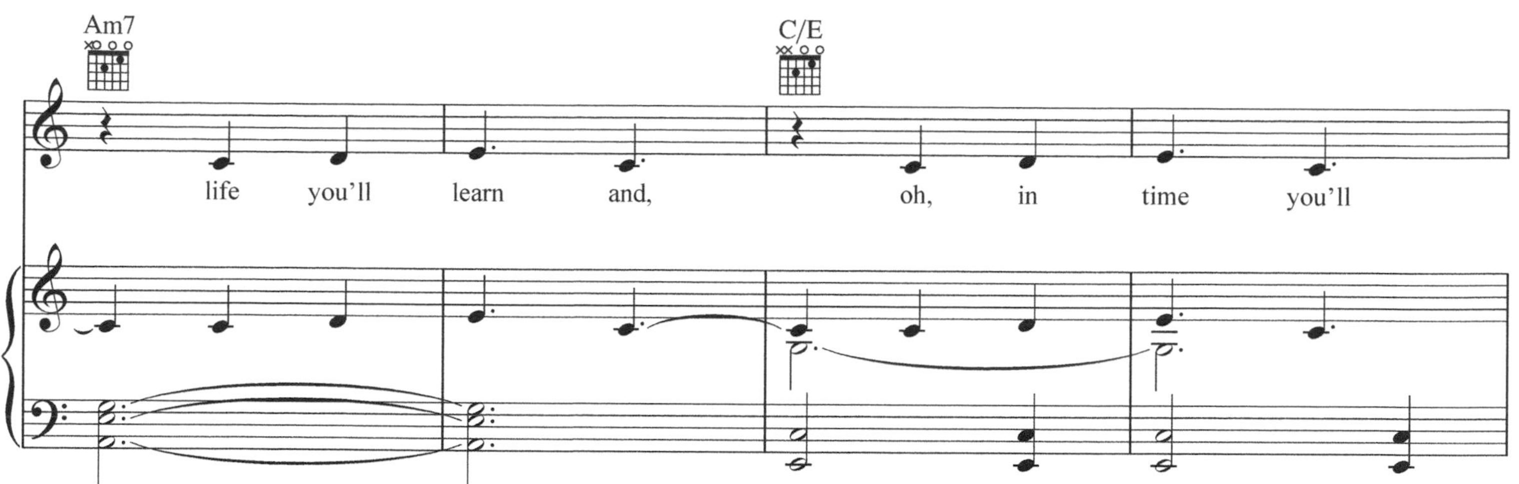
Am7
C/E
life you'll learn and, oh, in time you'll

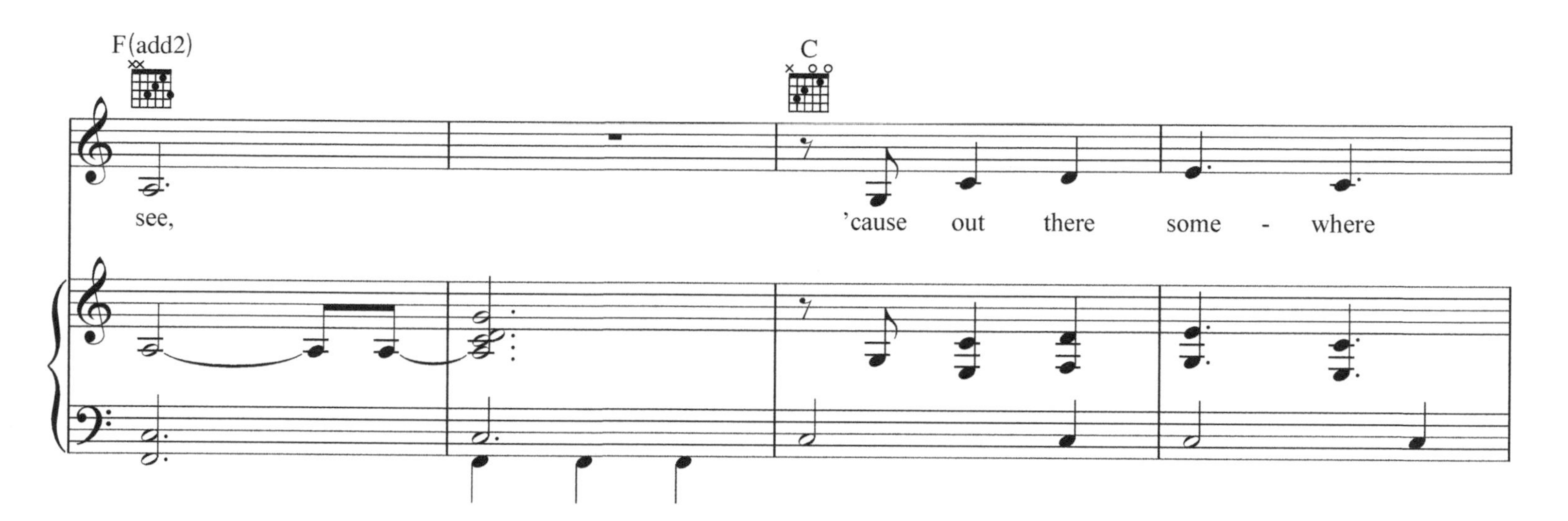
F(add2)
C
see, 'cause out there some - where

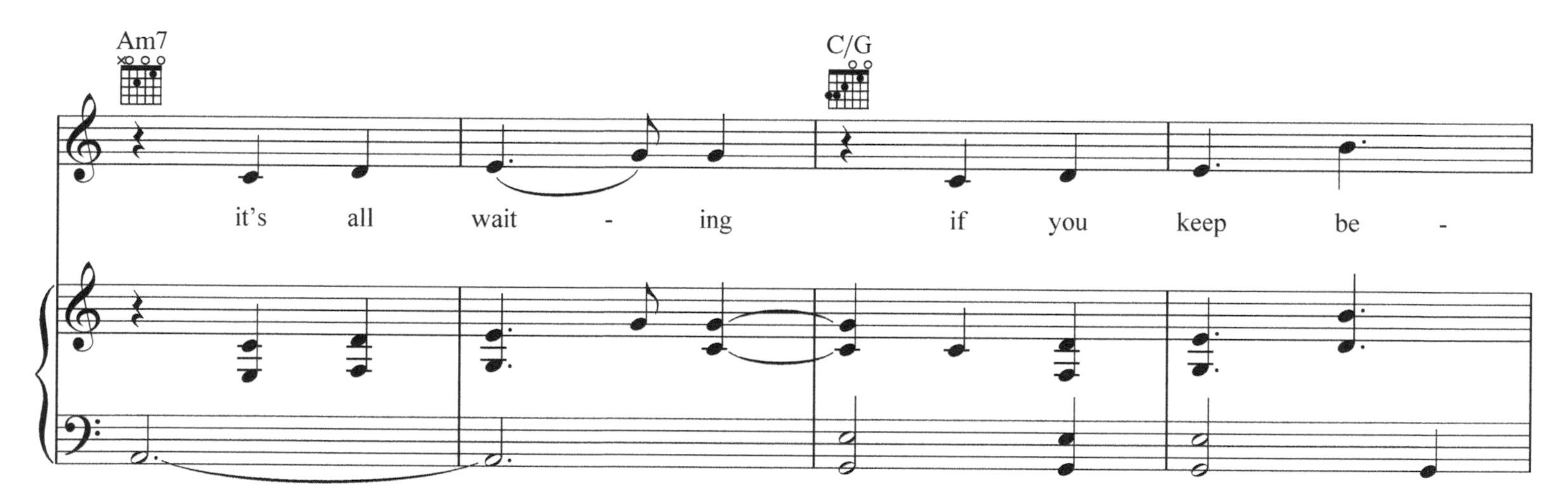
Am7
C/G
it's all wait - ing if you keep be -

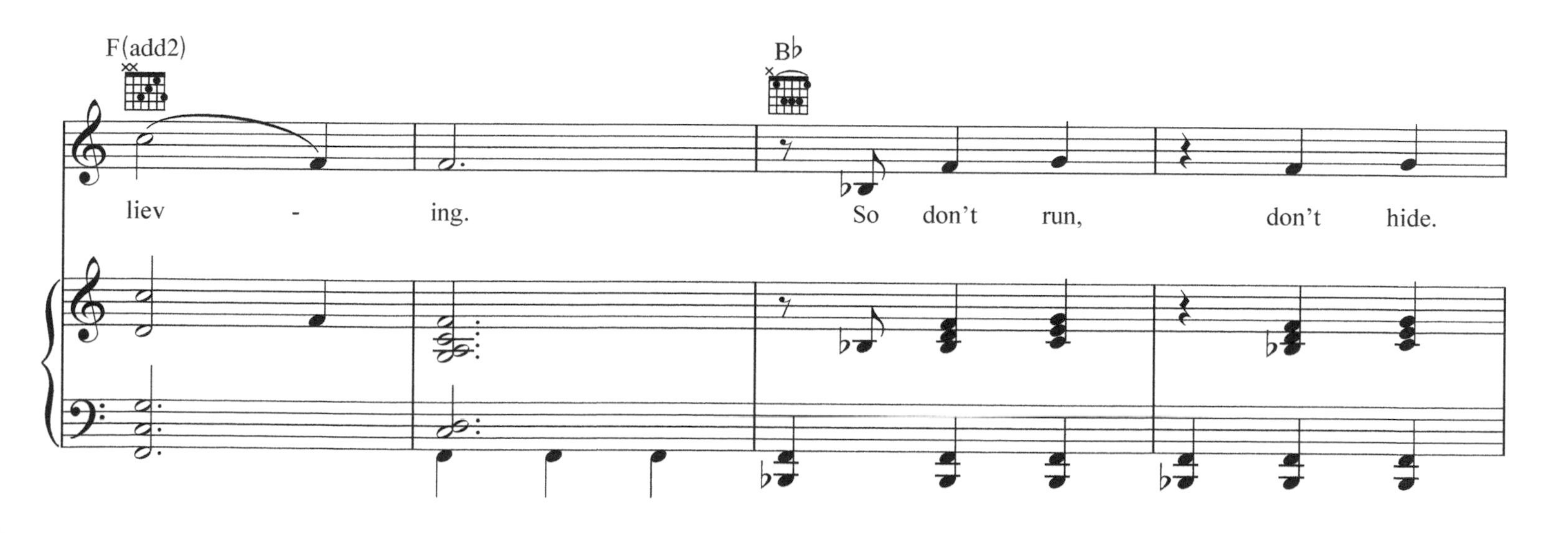
F(add2)
B♭
liev - ing. So don't run, don't hide.

C
B♭/D
It will be all right. You'll see; trust me.

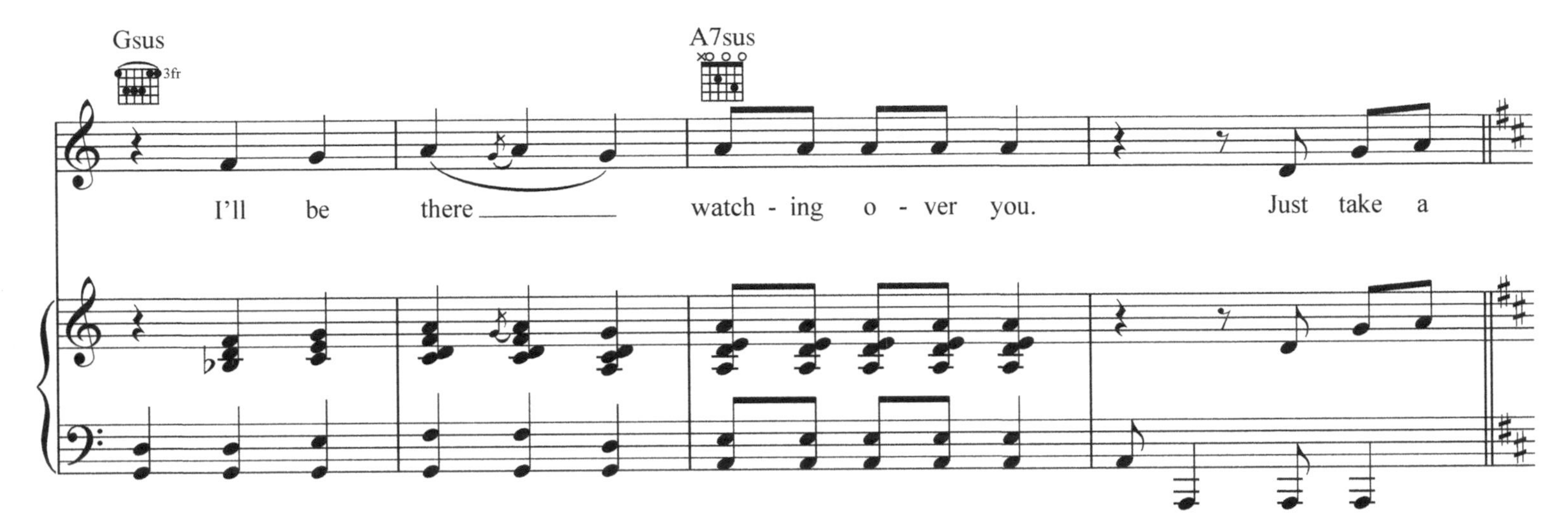
Gsus
3fr
A7sus
I'll be there watch - ing o - ver you. Just take a

D
D/F♯
Gsus2
D/F♯
look through my eyes.

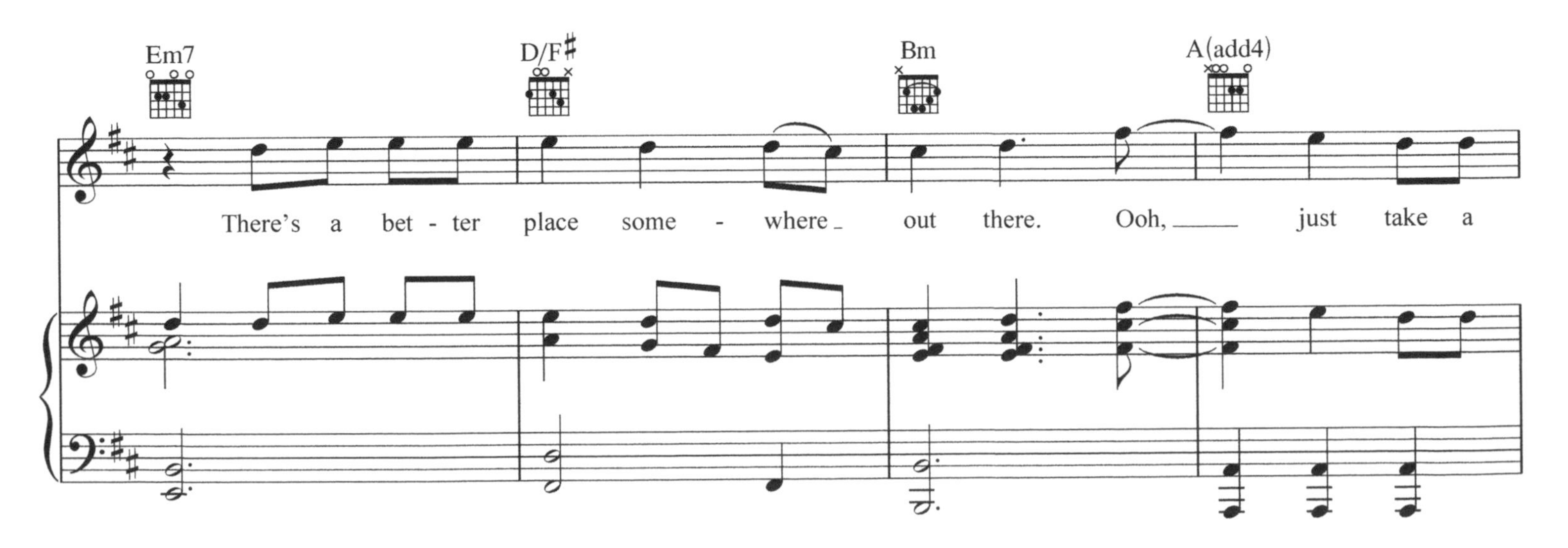
Em7
D/F♯
Bm
A(add4)
There's a bet - ter place some - where out there. Ooh, just take a

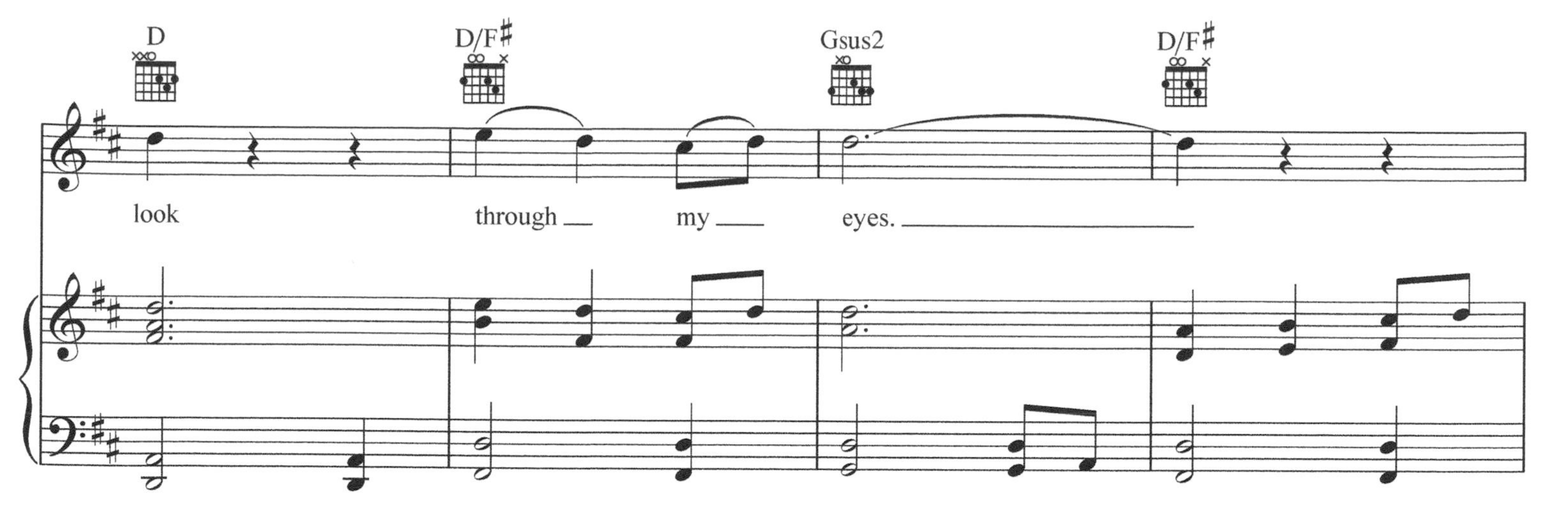
D
D/F♯
Gsus2
D/F♯
look through my eyes.

Em7
D/F♯
Bm7
A(add4)
Ev - 'ry - thing chang - es. You'll be a - mazed what you'll

G
A
find if you look through my

B
eyes.

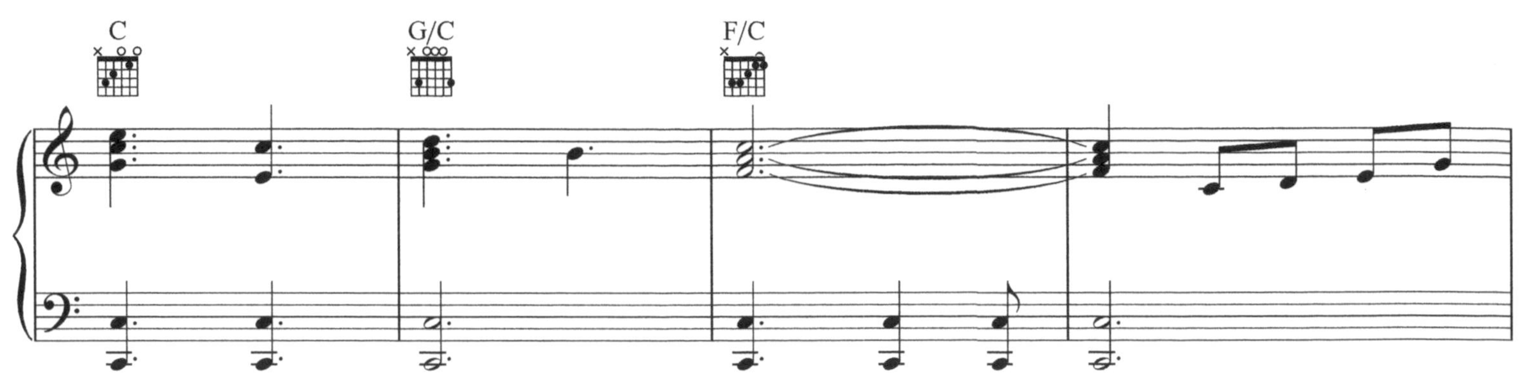
C
G/C
F/C

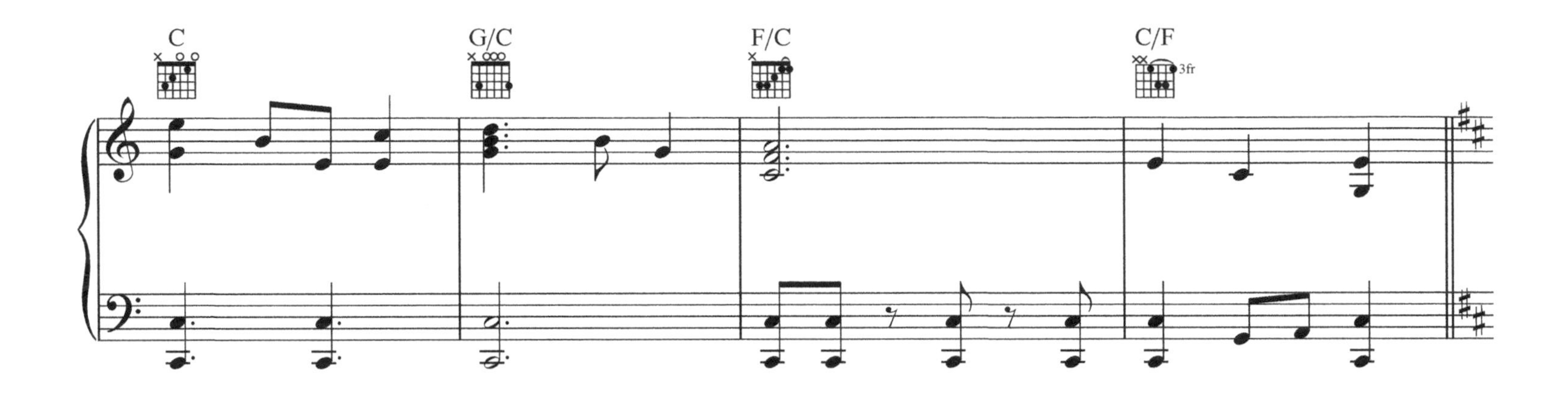
C
G/C
F/C
C/F
3fr

D
Bm7
There will be times on this jour - ney,

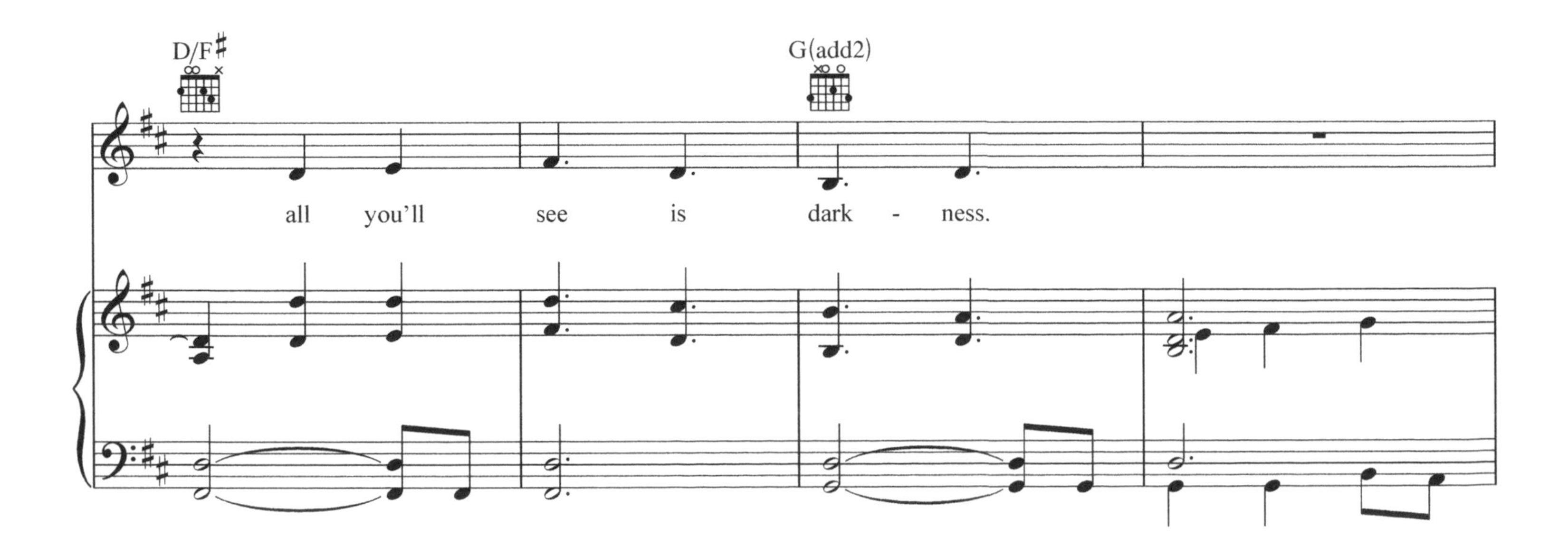
D/F#
G(add2)
all you'll see is dark - ness.

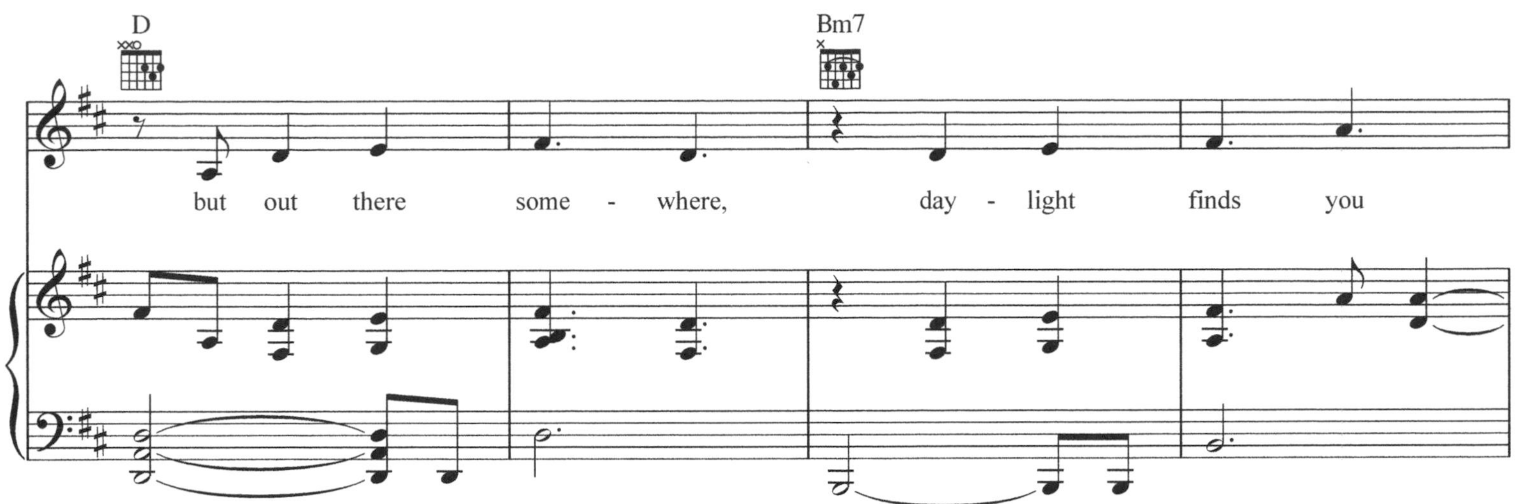
D
Bm7
but out there some - where, day - light finds you

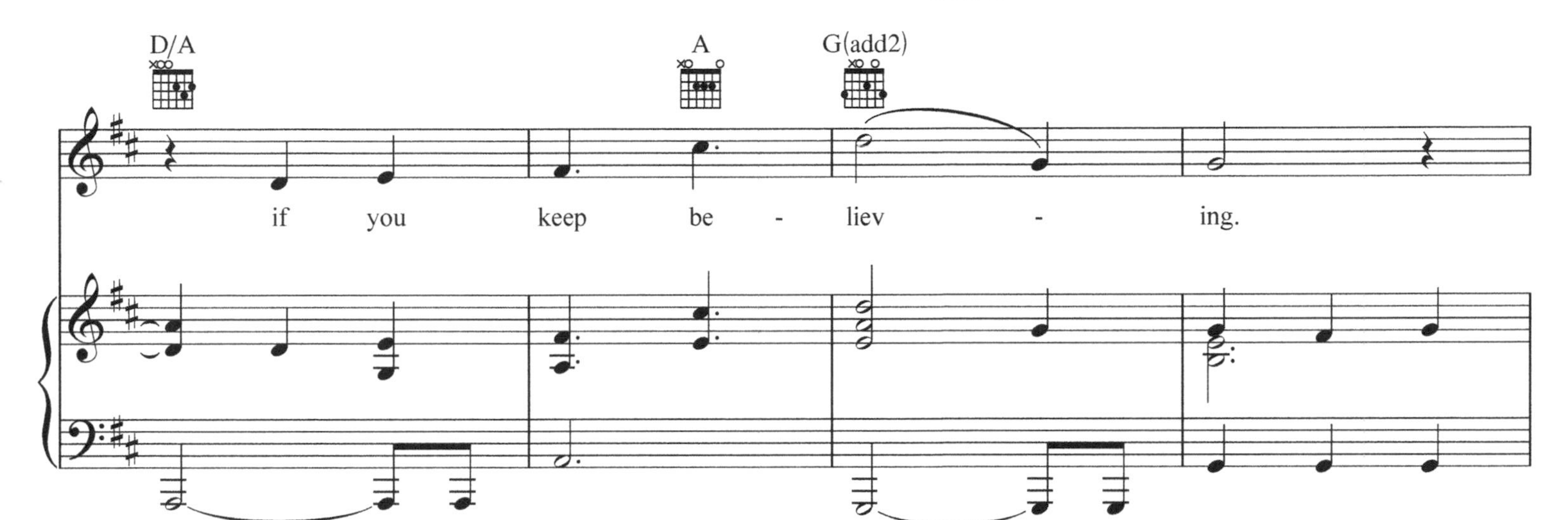
D/A
A
G(add2)
if you keep be - liev - ing.

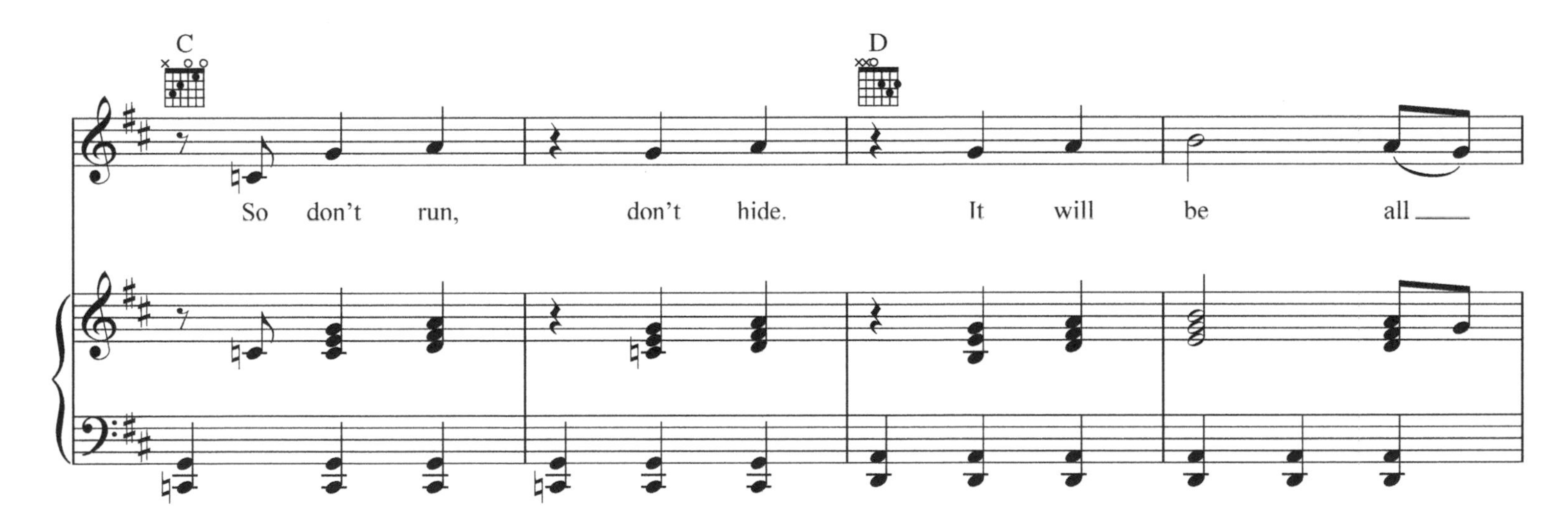
C
D
So don't run, don't hide. It will be all

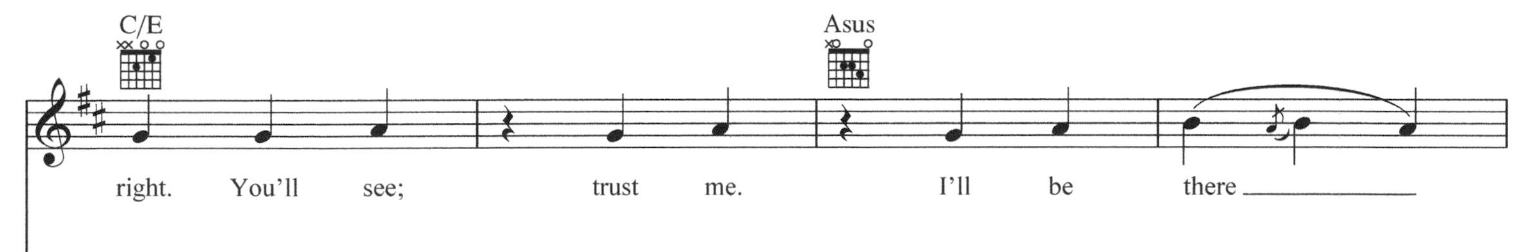
C/E
Asus
right. You'll see; trust me. I'll be there

B7sus
2fr
E
E/G♯
watch - ing o - ver you.
Just take a
look
through
my

Asus2
E/G♯
F♯m7
E/G♯
C♯m
4fr
eyes.
There's a bet - ter place some - where out there.

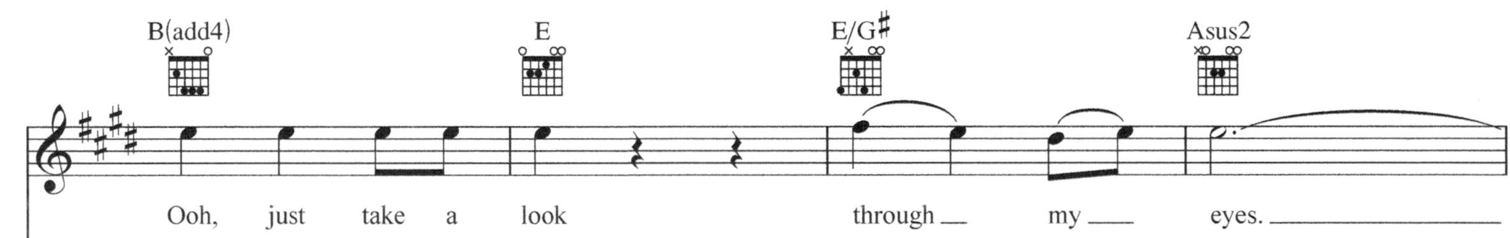
B(add4)
E
E/G♯
Asus2
Ooh, just take a look
through
my
eyes.

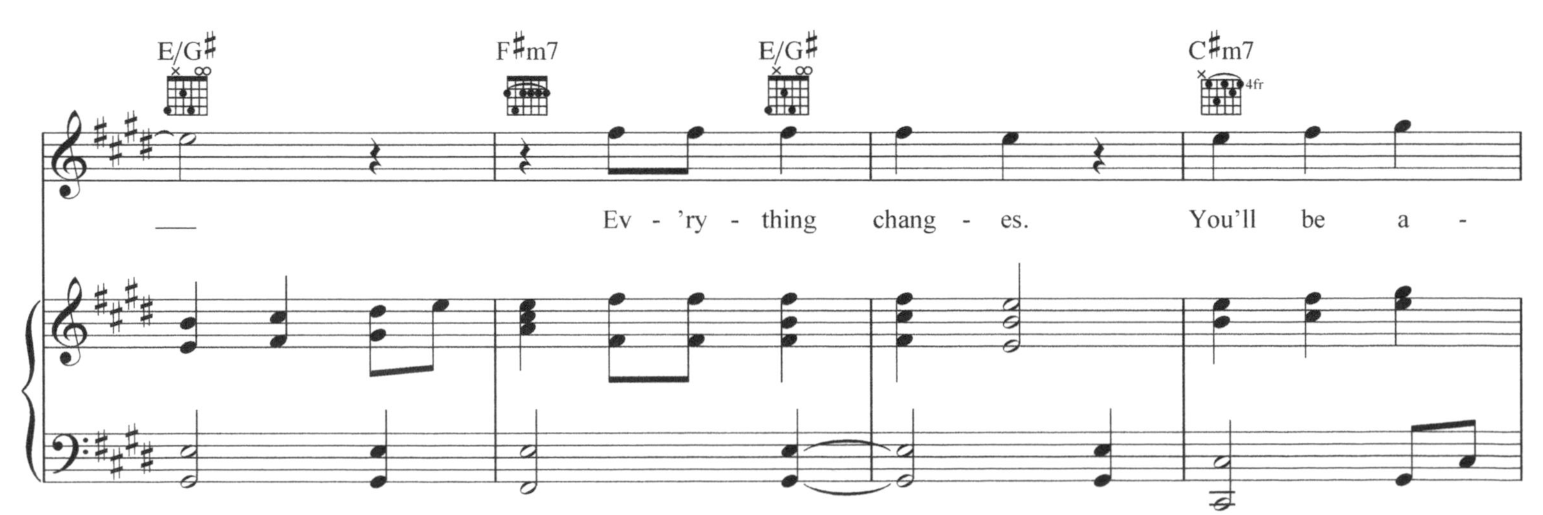
E/G♯
F♯m7
E/G♯
C♯m7
4fr
Ev - 'ry - thing chang - es.
You'll be a -

B(add4)
A
C♭
mazed what you'll find
if you look through my __

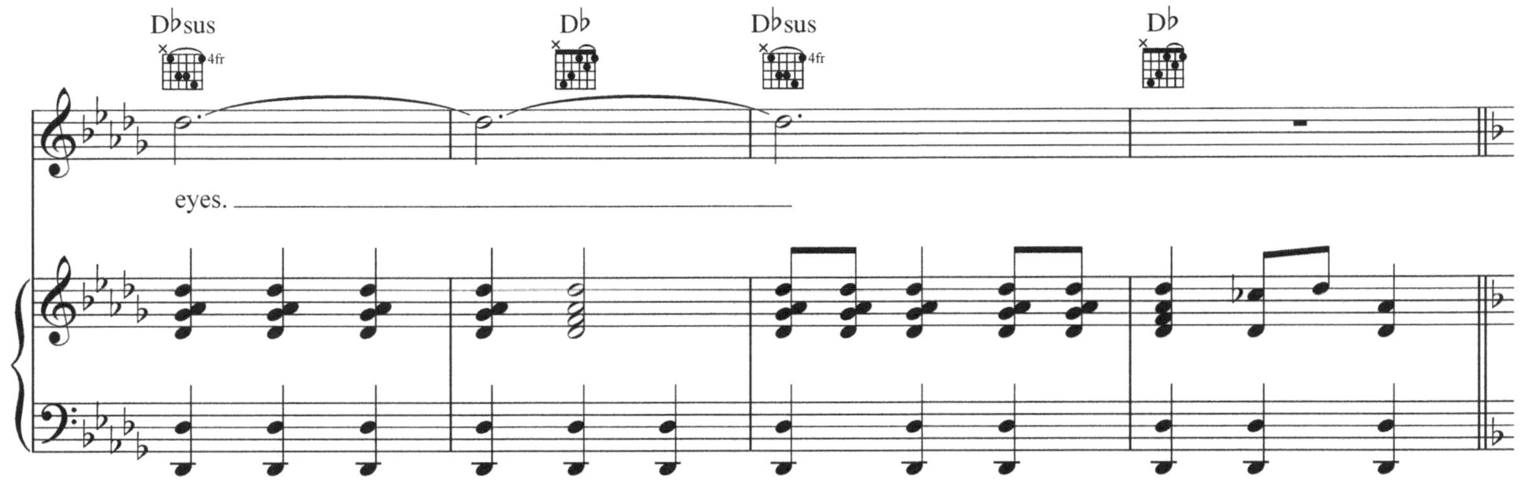
D♭sus
4fr
D♭
D♭sus
4fr
D♭
eyes. __

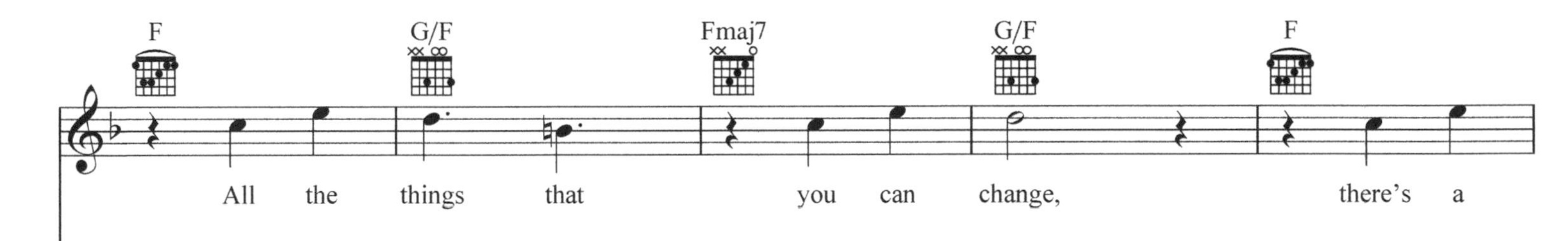
F
G/F
Fmaj7
G/F
F
All the things that you can change, there's a

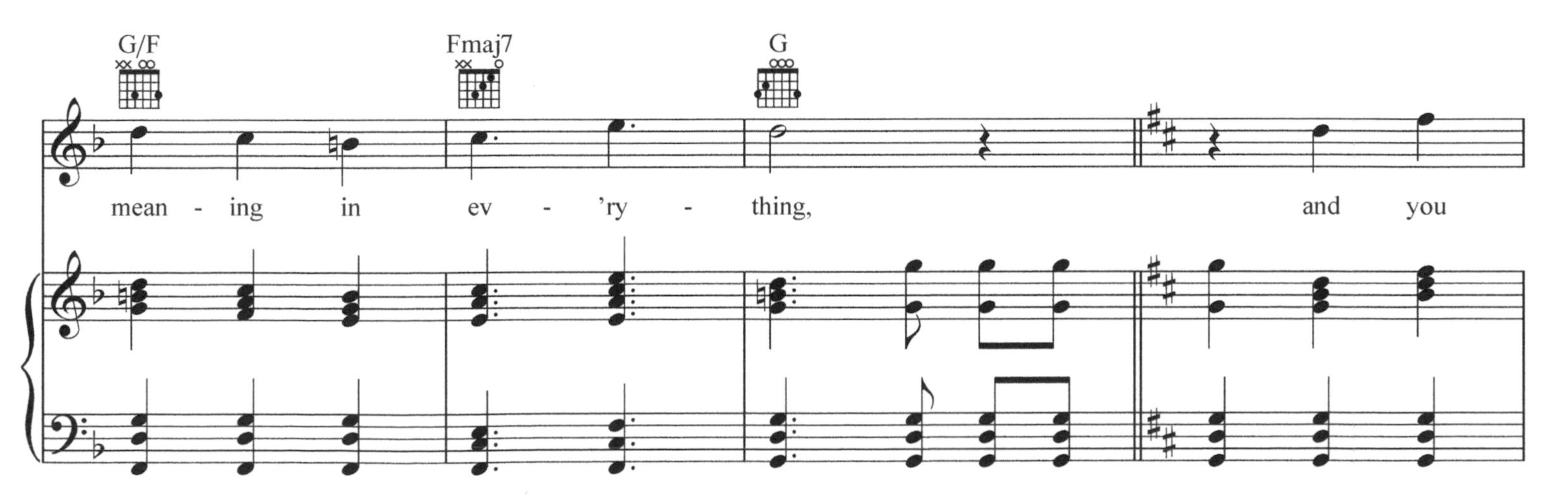
G/F
Fmaj7
G
mean - ing in ev - 'ry - thing, and you

A/G
G
A/G
G
will find all you need. There's so
A/G
G
B
E
much to un - der - stand. Take a look
E/G♯
Asus2
E/G♯
F♯m7
through my eyes. There's a bet - ter
E/G♯
C♯m
4fr
B(add4)
E
place some - where out there. Ooh, just take a look

E/G♯
Asus2
E/G♯
F♯m7
E/G♯
through my eyes.
Ev - 'ry - thing chang - es.
C♯m7
4fr
B(add4)
1
A
You'll be a - mazed what you'll find.
Oh,
just take a
2
A
B
find. (You'll find a bet - ter place) if you
A/C♯
B/D♯
4fr
look through my eyes. (You know there's a bet - ter place.) Just take a

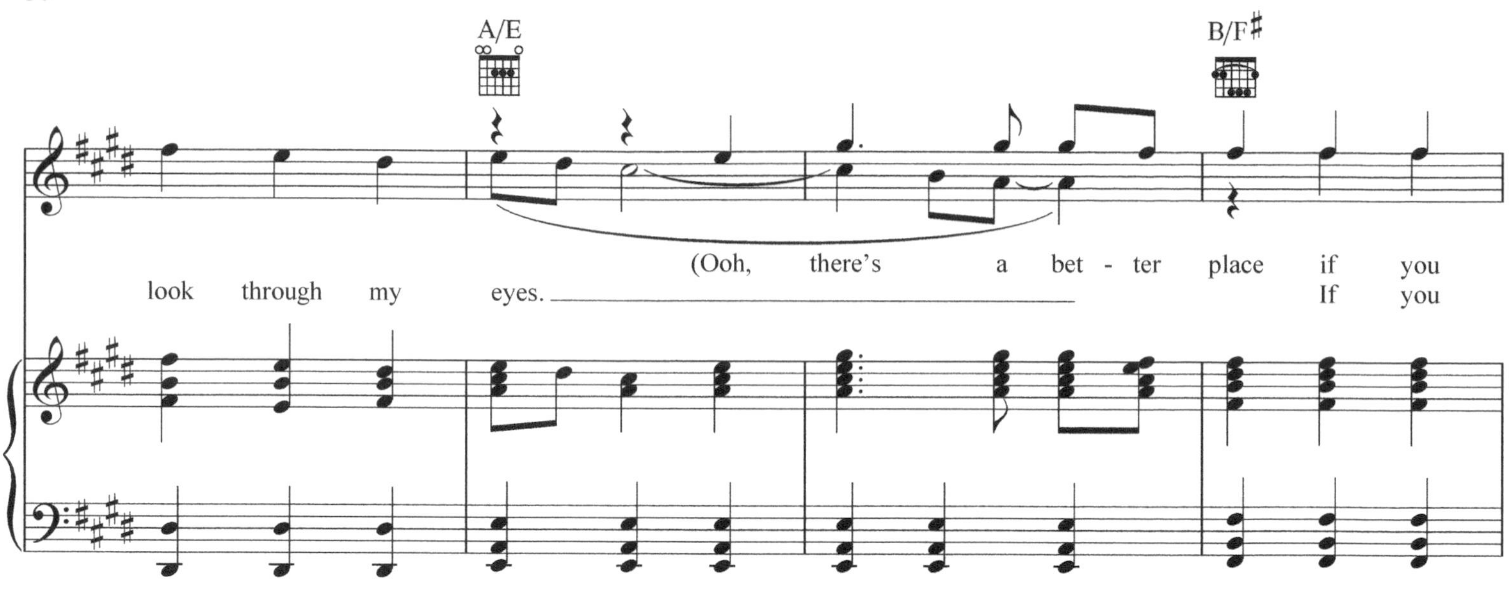
A/E
B/F♯
(Ooh, there's a bet - ter place if you
look through my eyes.
If you

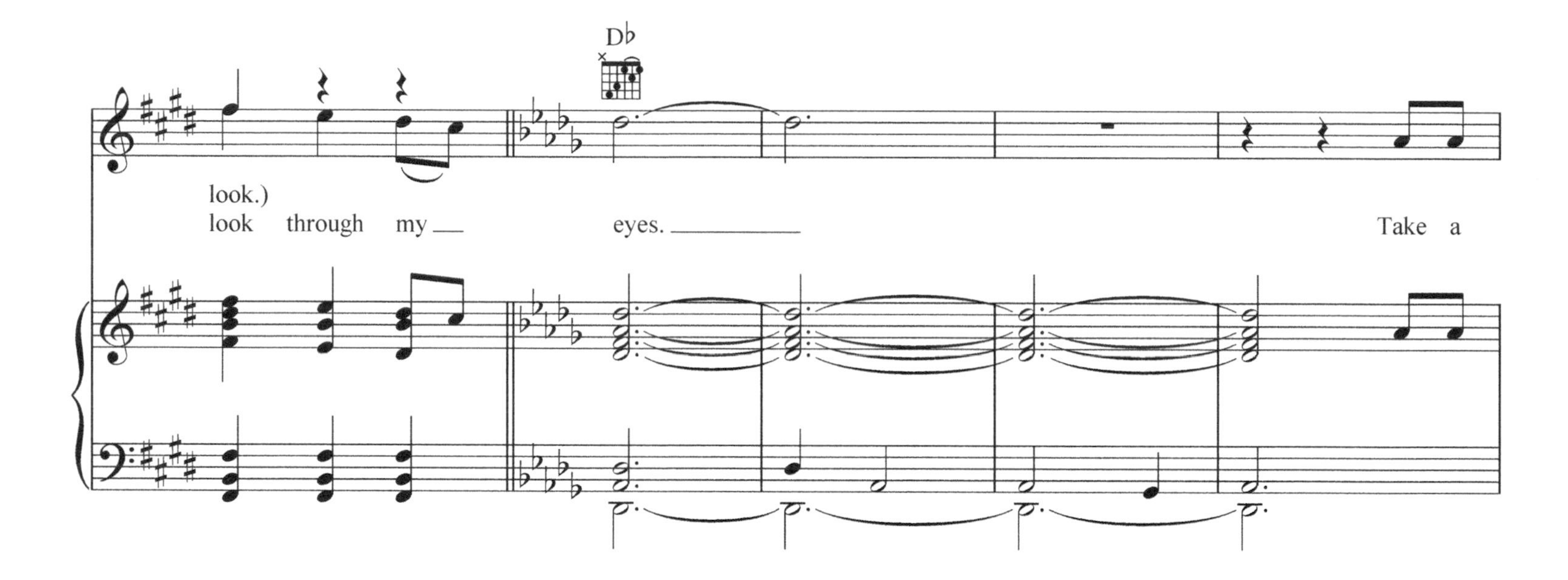
D♭
look.)
look through my eyes.
Take a

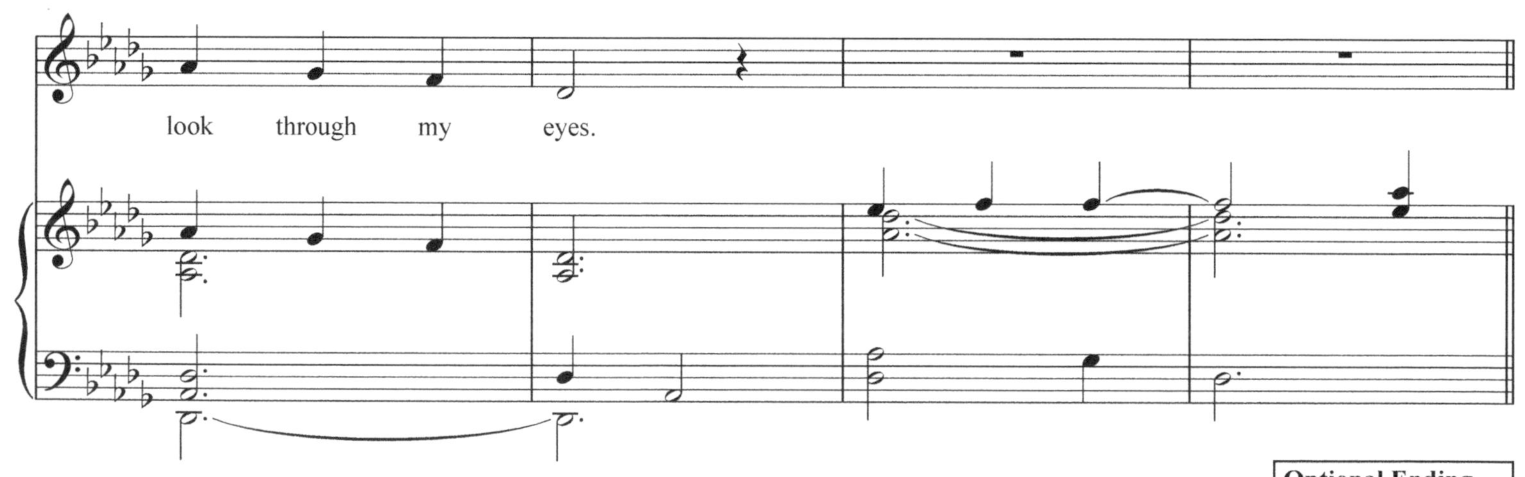
look through my eyes.

D♭
Repeat and Fade
Optional Ending

YOU'LL BE IN MY HEART
(Pop Version)
from Walt Disney Pictures' TARZAN™
as performed by Phil Collins

Words and Music by
PHIL COLLINS

C♯/F♯
F♯
4fr
seem so strong. My arms will hold you, keep you
way we feel? They just don't trust what they

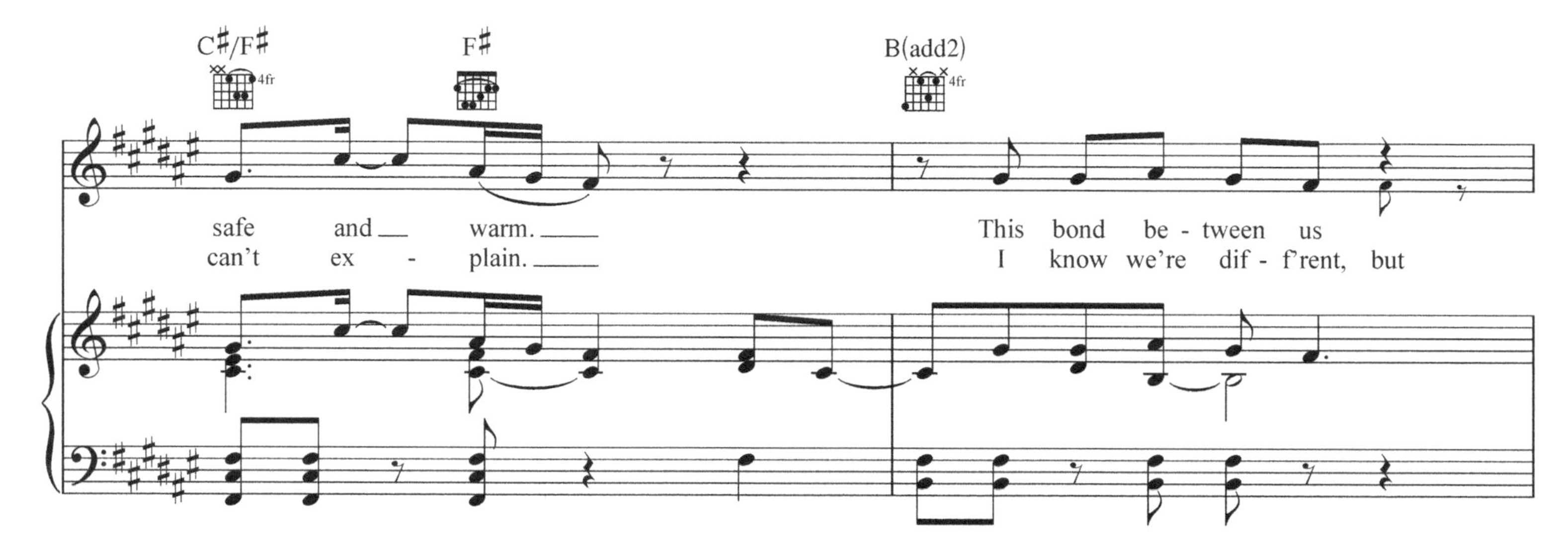
C♯/F♯
F♯
B(add2)
4fr
safe and warm. This bond be - tween us
can't ex - plain. I know we're dif - f'rent, but

G♯m
C♯
B♭
4fr
can't be bro - ken. I will be here; don't you cry. 'Cause
deep in - side us we're not that dif-fer-ent at all. And

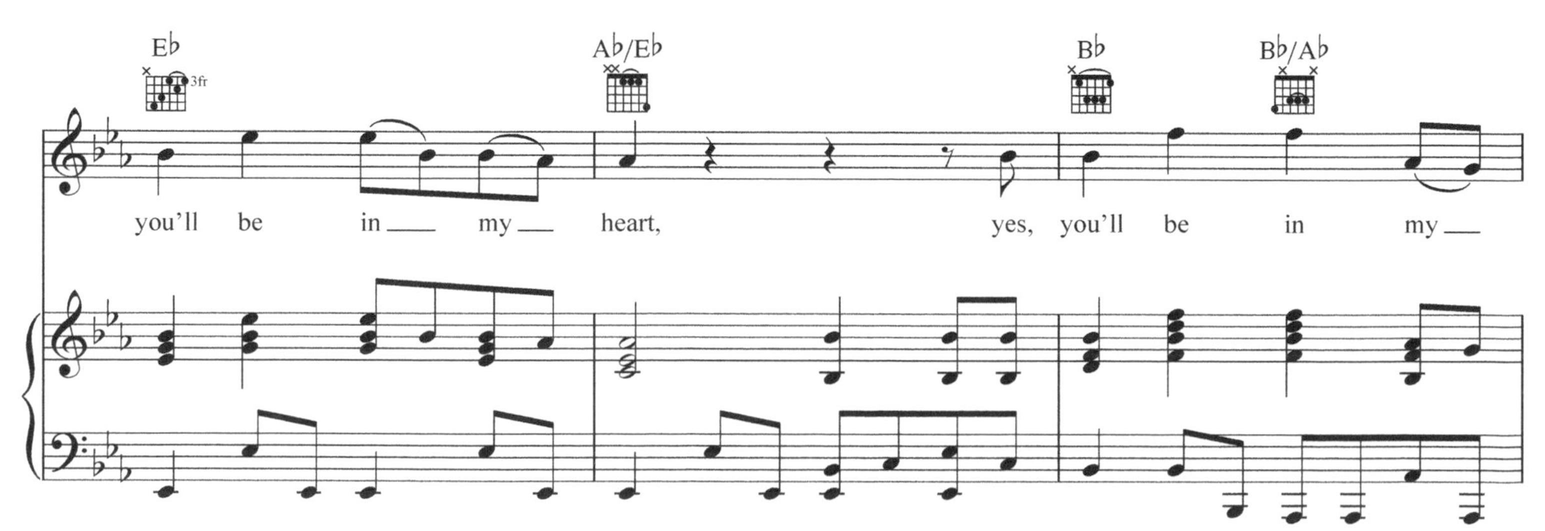
E♭
A♭/E♭
B♭
B♭/A♭
3fr
you'll be in my heart, yes, you'll be in my

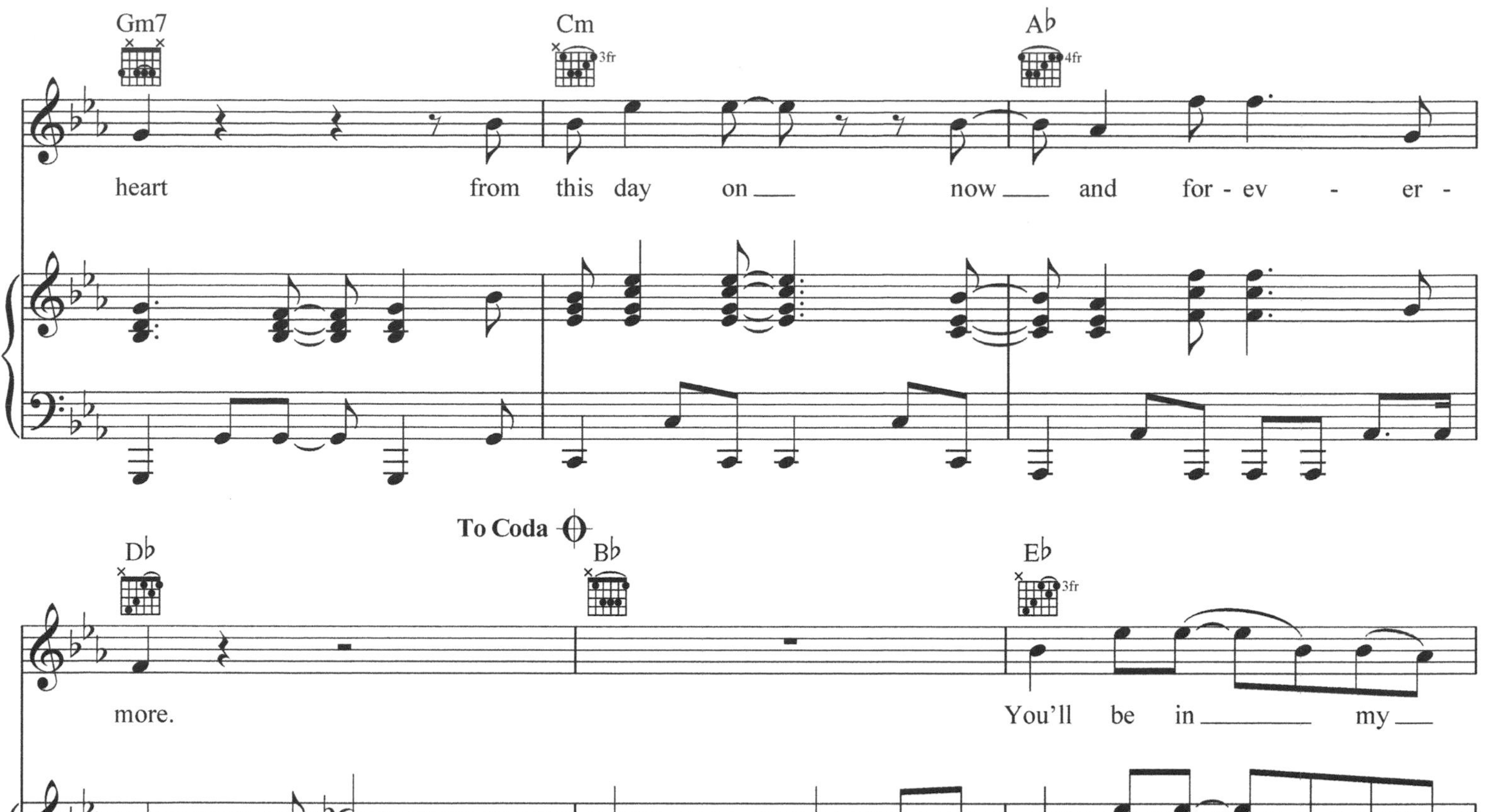
Gm7
Cm
A♭
3fr
4fr
heart from this day on now and for - ev - er -
To Coda
D♭
B♭
E♭
3fr
more. You'll be in my

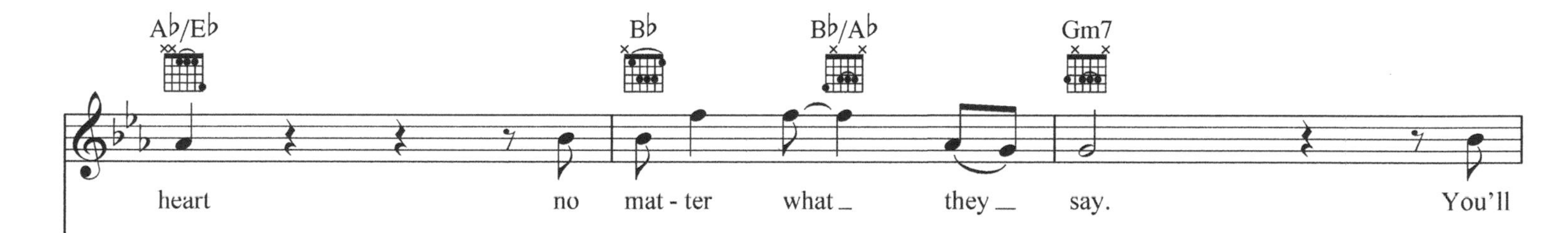
A♭/E♭
B♭
B♭/A♭
Gm7
heart no mat - ter what they say. You'll

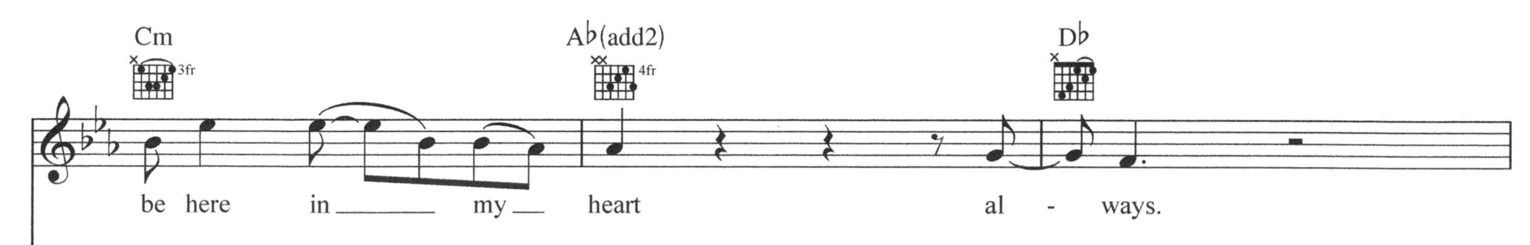
Cm
A♭(add2)
D♭
3fr
4fr
be here in my heart al - ways.

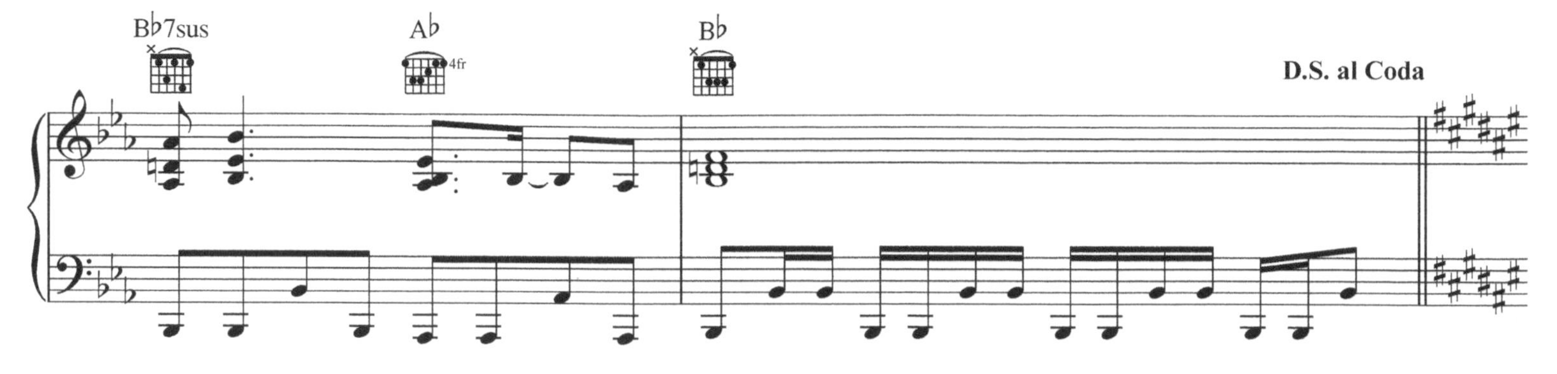
B♭7sus
A♭
4fr
B♭
D.S. al Coda

CODA
B♭
A♭sus
4fr
A♭
4fr
Don't
lis - ten to them, 'cause
des - ti - ny calls you, you

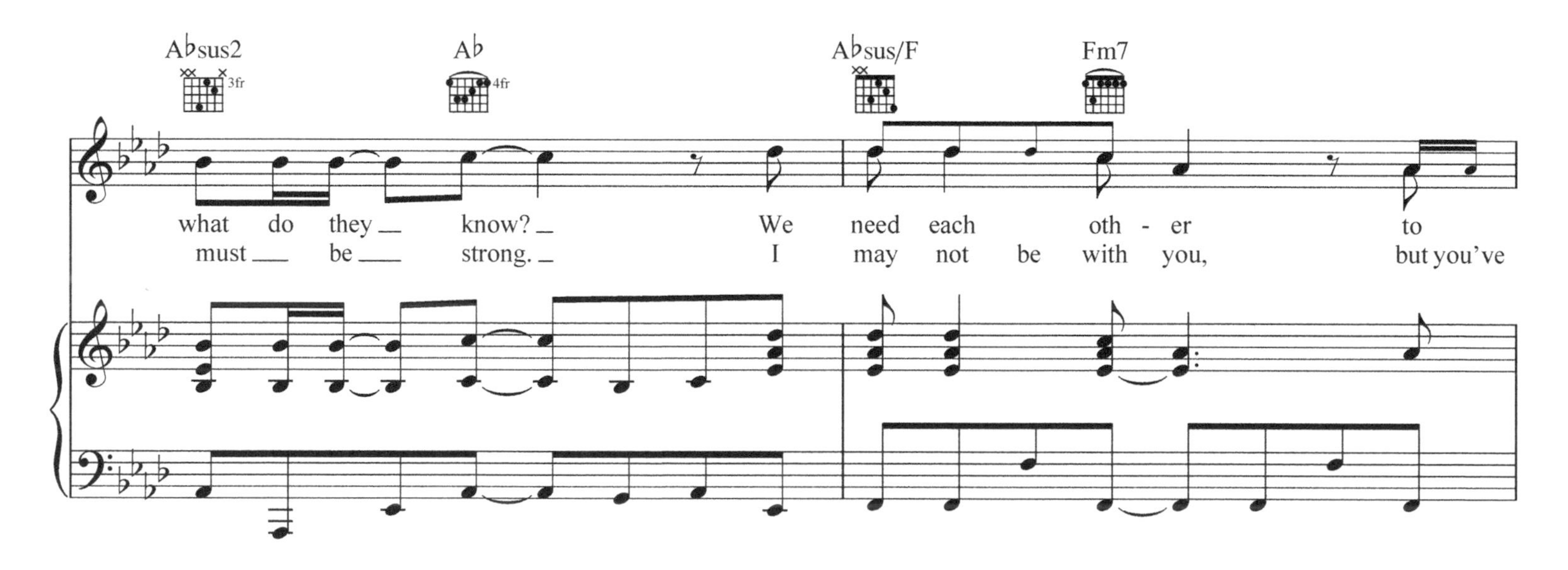
A♭sus2
3fr
A♭
4fr
A♭sus/F
Fm7
what do they know? We need each oth - er to
must be strong. I may not be with you, but you've

A♭sus2/F
Fm7
Cm7
3fr
have, to hold.
got to hold on.
They'll see in time, I

1
2
D♭
D♭
know.
When
know.
We'll

E♭
B♭
F
B♭/F
show them to-geth-er, 'cause
you'll be in my
heart.
Be-lieve me,

C
C/B♭
Am7
Dm
you'll be in my
heart.
I'll be there from this day on,
now

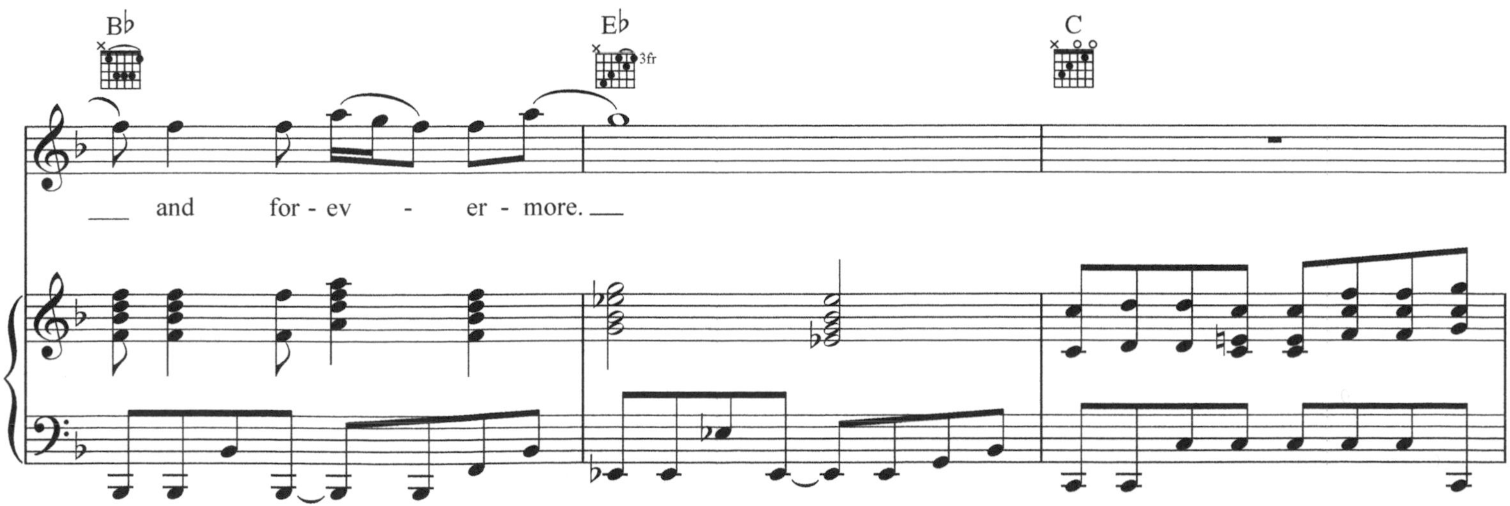
B♭
E♭
C
and for-ev-er-more.

F
B♭/F
C
C/B♭
(You'll be here in my heart.)
You'll be in my heart no mat-ter what they

Am
Dm
B♭(add2)
3fr
(I'll be with you.)
say. You'll be here in my heart (I'll be there.) al-

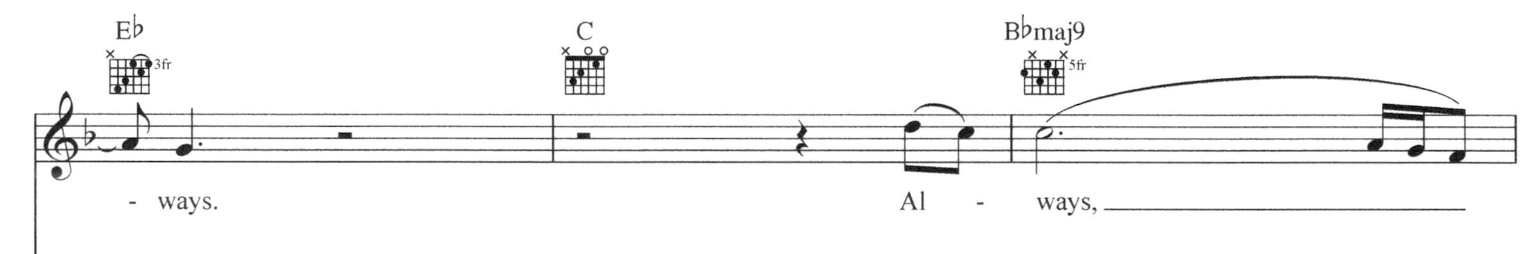
E♭
3fr
C
B♭maj9
5fr
- ways. Al - ways,

F(add2)
I'll be with you. I'll be

B♭maj9
5fr
F(add2)
there for you al - ways,
al - ways and al - ways.

B♭maj9
5fr
Just look o - ver your shoul - der.
Just look o -

F(add2)
B♭maj9
5fr
- ver your shoul - der.
Just look o - ver your shoul - der;

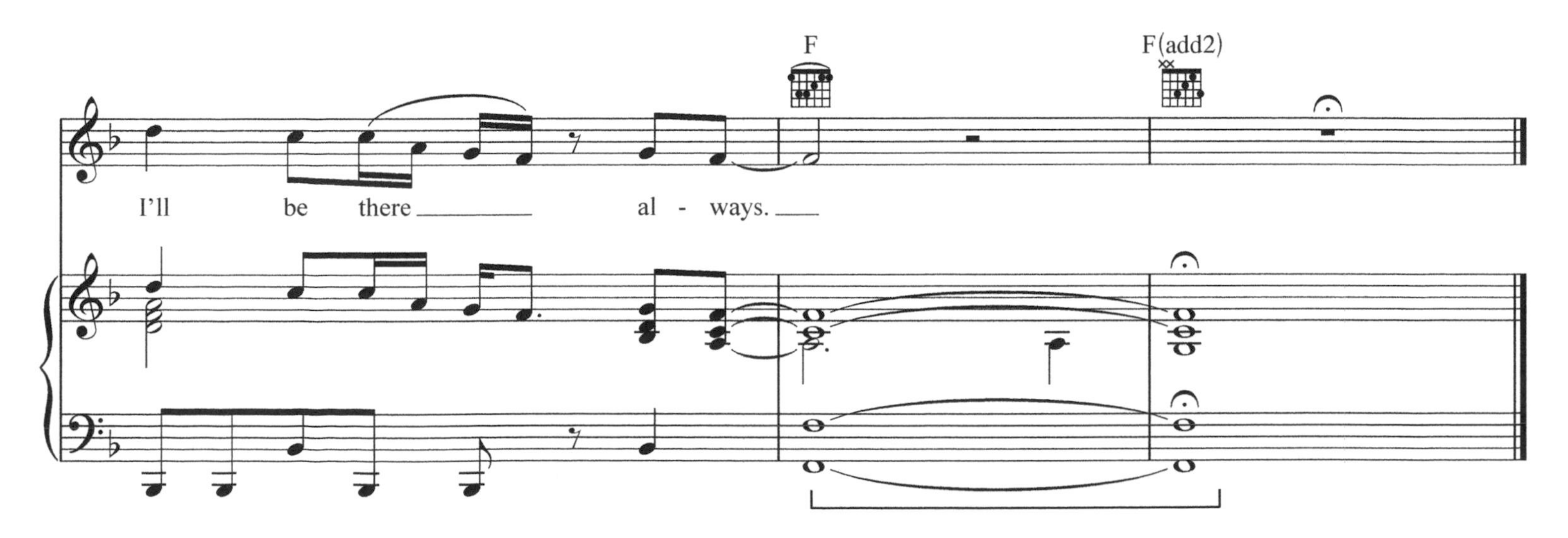

F
F(add2)
I'll be there al - ways.

A WHOLE NEW WORLD

from Disney ALADDIN

Music by ALAN MENKEN
Lyrics by TIM RICE

Sweetly

D(add9)

mf

D

I can show _ you the world,

G/B A/C♯ Em/G F♯7 F♯7/A♯

shin - ing, shim - mer - ing, splen - did. Tell me, prin - cess, now

Bm Bm/A G D A7sus

when did you last let your heart _ de - cide? _

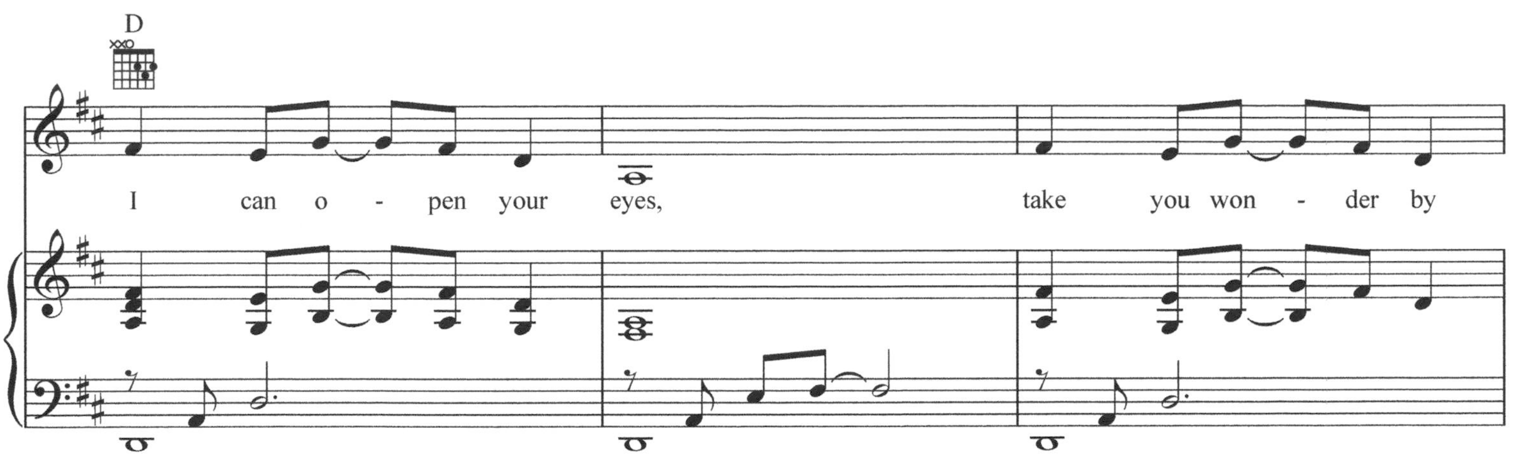
D
I can o - pen your eyes, take you won - der by

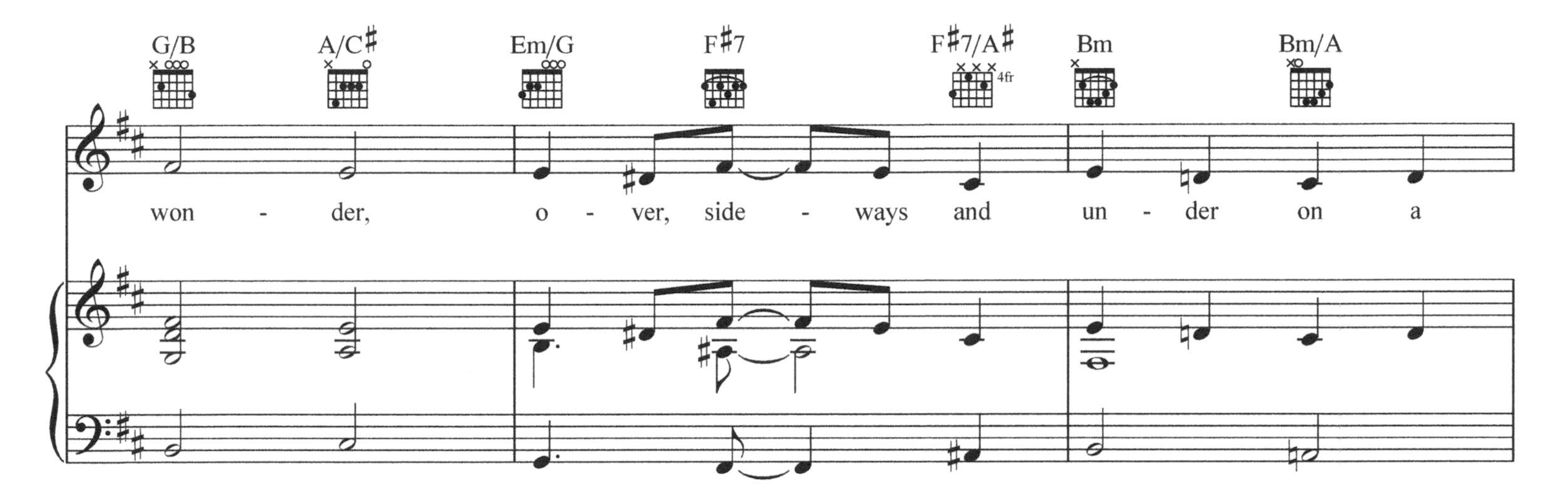
G/B A/C♯ Em/G F♯7 F♯7/A♯ Bm Bm/A
4fr
won - der, o - ver, side - ways and un - der on a

G D A
mag - ic car - pet ride. A whole new world,

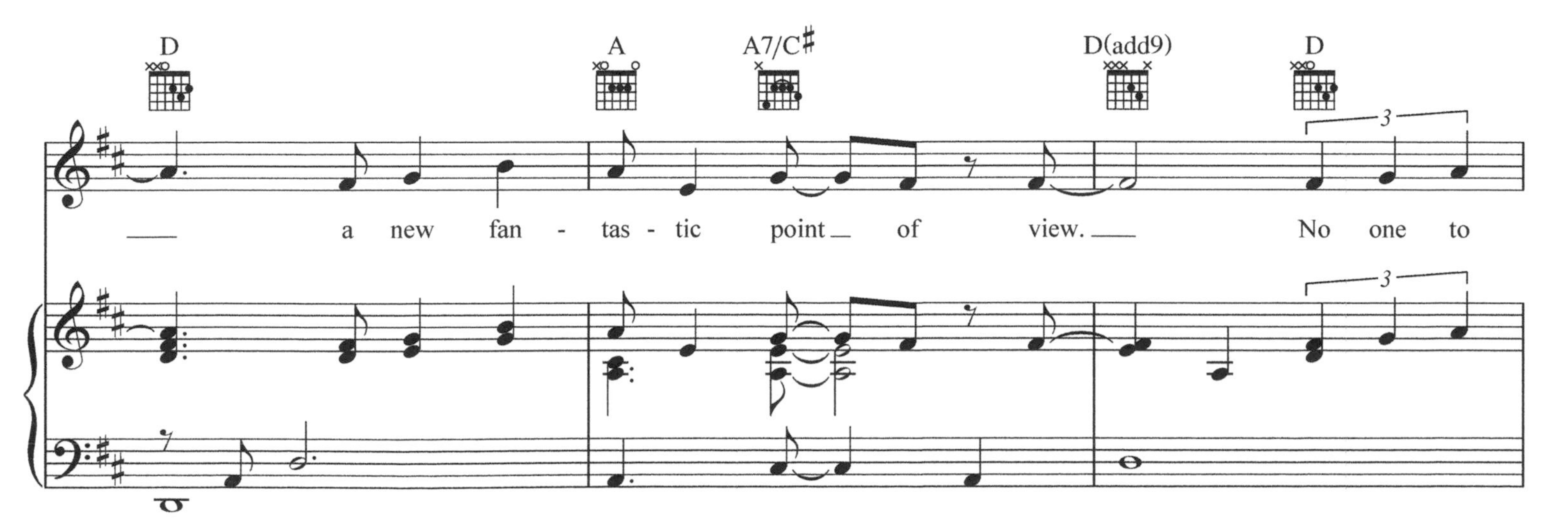
D A A7/C♯ D(add9) D
a new fan - tas - tic point of view. No one to
3

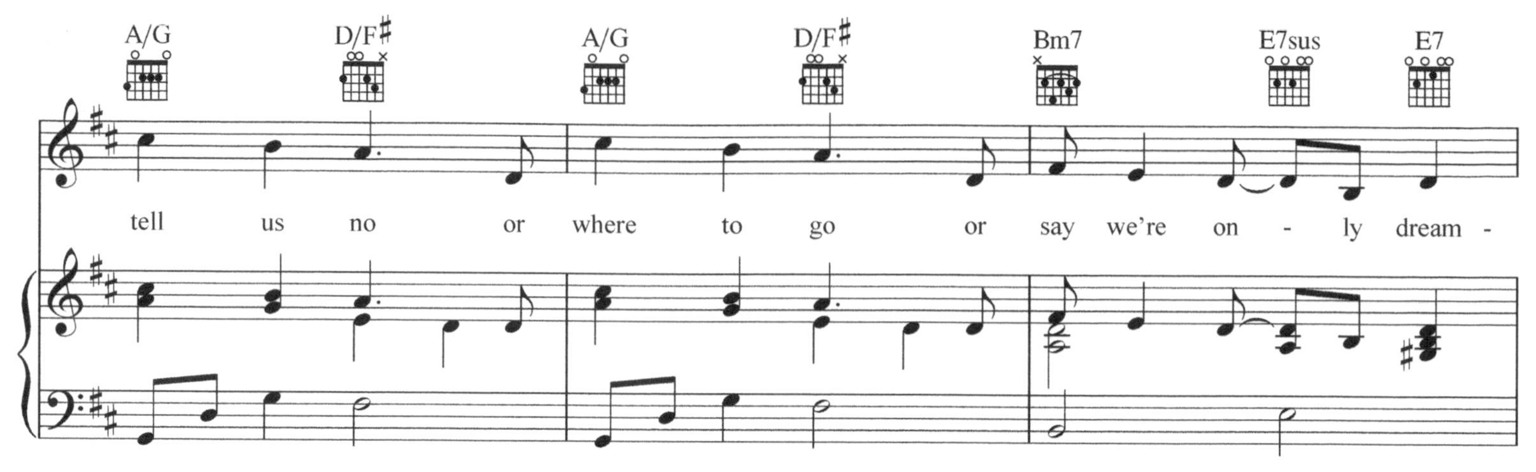
A/G
D/F♯
A/G
D/F♯
Bm7
E7sus
E7
tell us no or where to go or say we're on - ly dream -

G/A
3fr
A
D
ing. A whole new world, a daz - zling

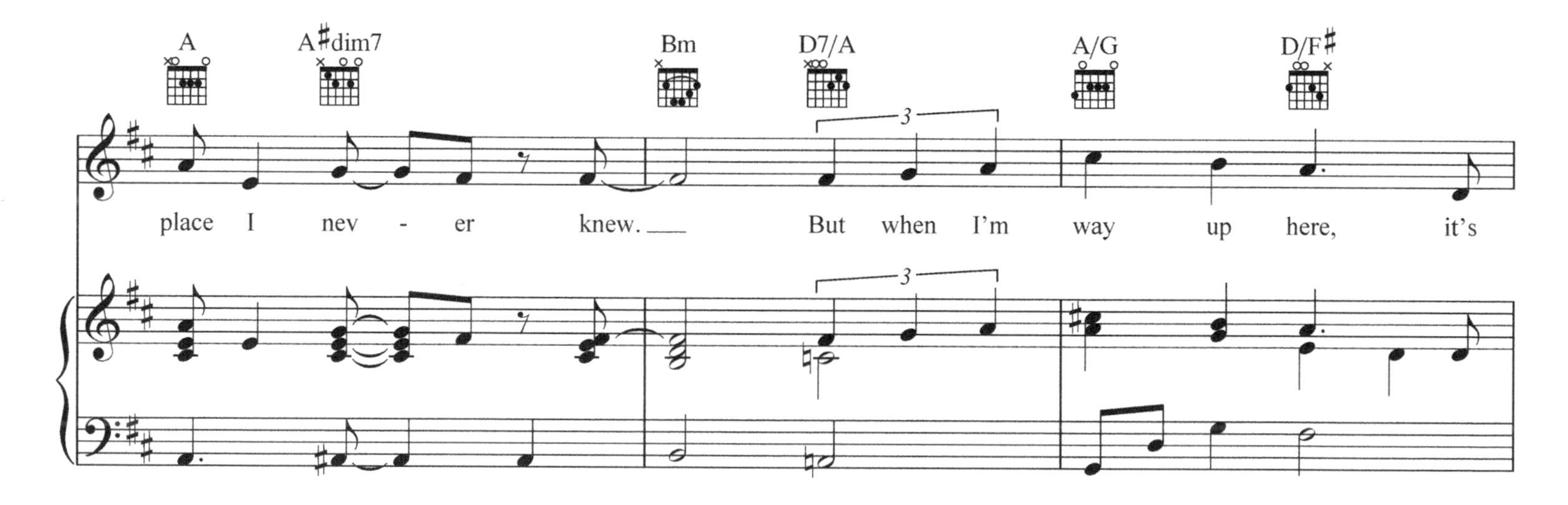
A
A♯dim7
Bm
D7/A
A/G
D/F♯
place I nev - er knew. But when I'm way up here, it's
3

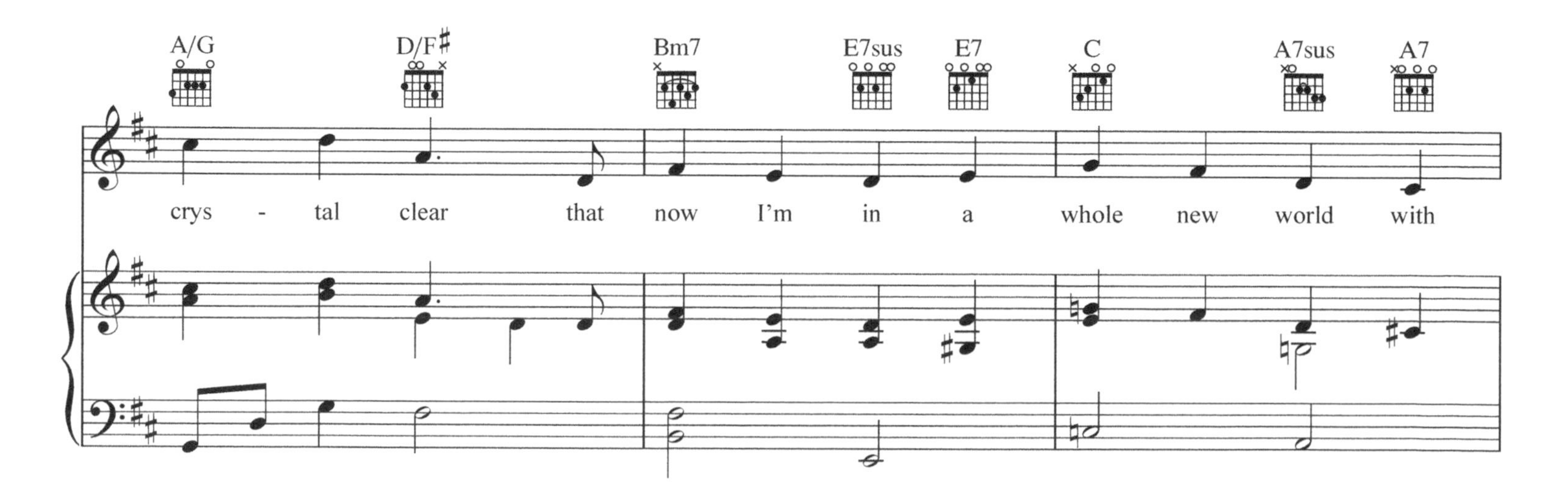
A/G
D/F♯
Bm7
E7sus
E7
C
A7sus
A7
crys - tal clear that now I'm in a whole new world with

D
F
you.
Un - be - liev - a - ble

B♭/D
C/E
sights,
in - de - scrib - a - ble feel - ing.

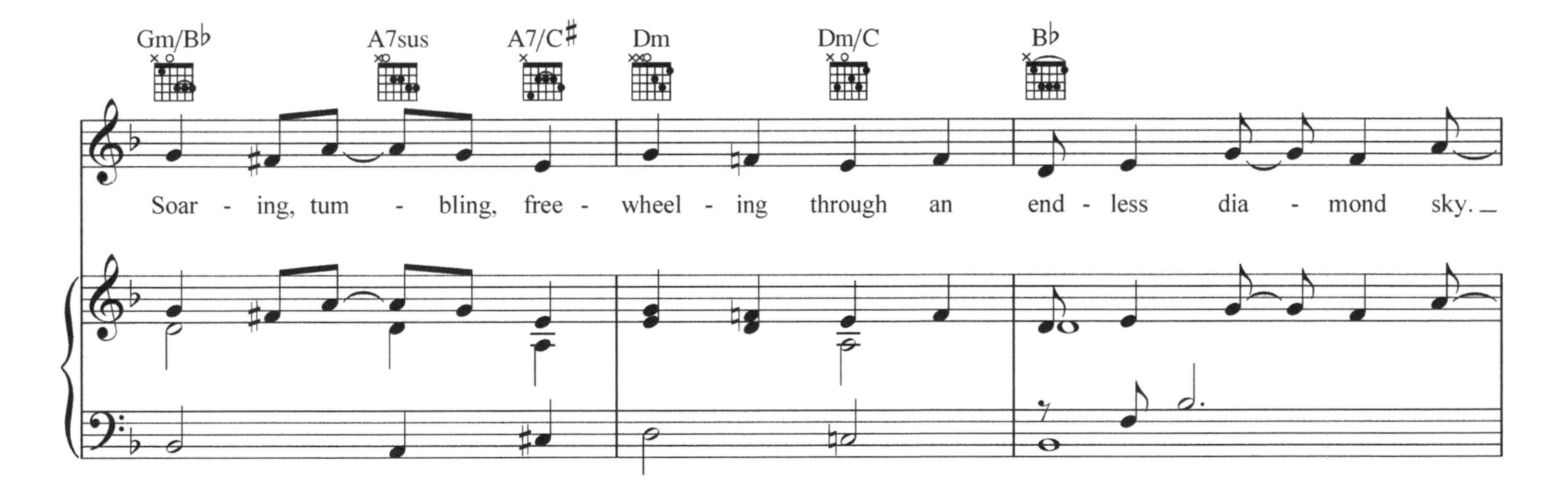
Gm/B♭
A7sus
A7/C♯
Dm
Dm/C
B♭
Soar - ing, tum - bling, free - wheel - ing through an end - less dia - mond sky.

F
C
F
A whole new world, a hun - dred

C
F
C/B♭
F/A
thou - sand things be - gin. I'm like a shoot - ing star, I've

C/B♭
F/A
Dm7
G7sus
G7
B♭/C
come so far; I can't go back. I'm in a whole new

C
F
C
C♯dim7
world with new ho - ri - zons to pur - sue.

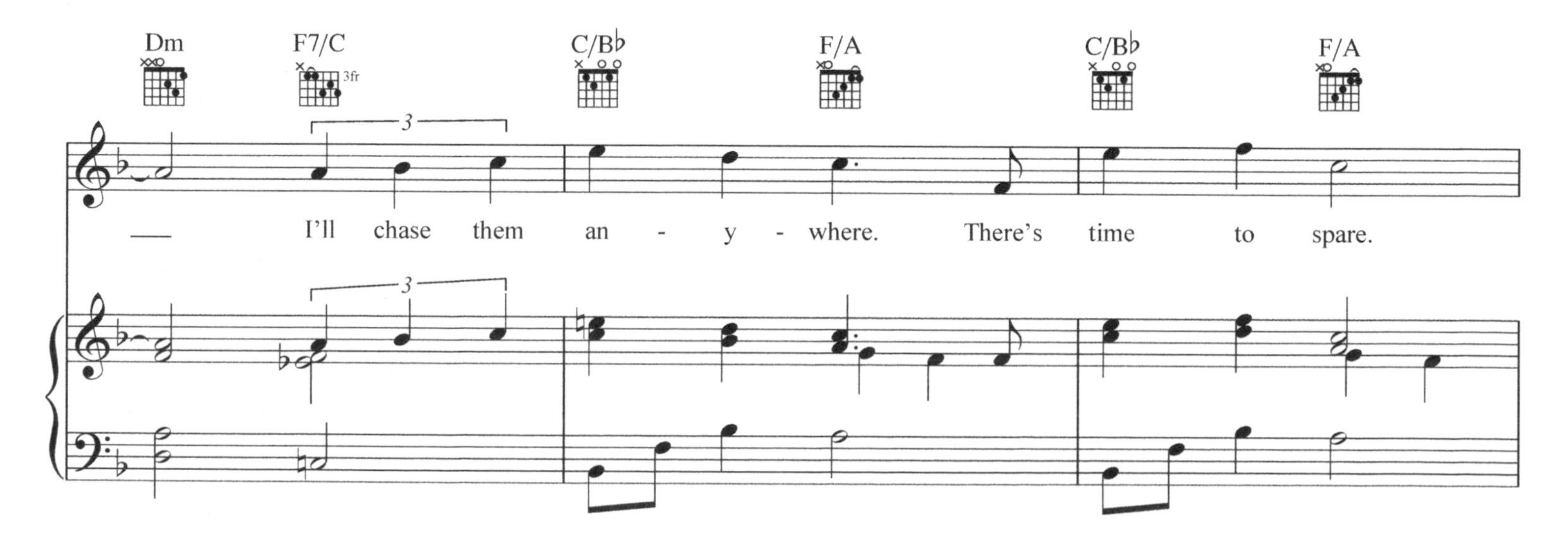
Dm
F7/C
3fr
C/B♭
F/A
C/B♭
F/A
I'll chase them an - y - where. There's time to spare.

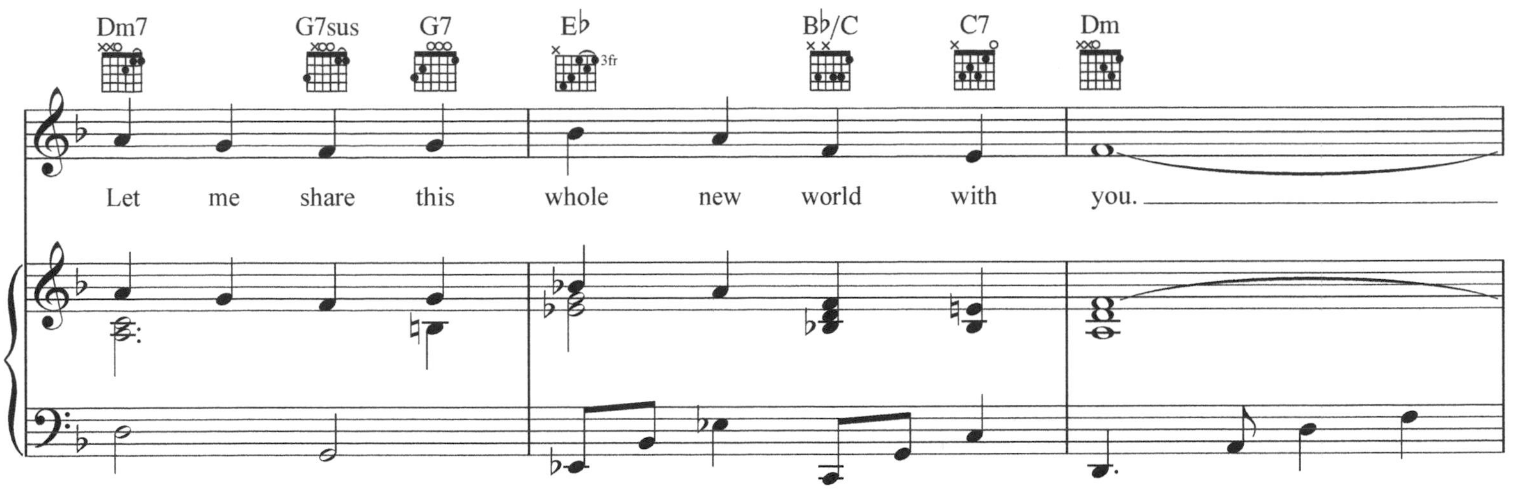
Dm7
G7sus
G7
E♭
3fr
B♭/C
C7
Dm
Let me share this whole new world with you.

F/C
B♭(add9)
6fr
F/A
Gm7(add4)
A whole new world, that's where we'll be.

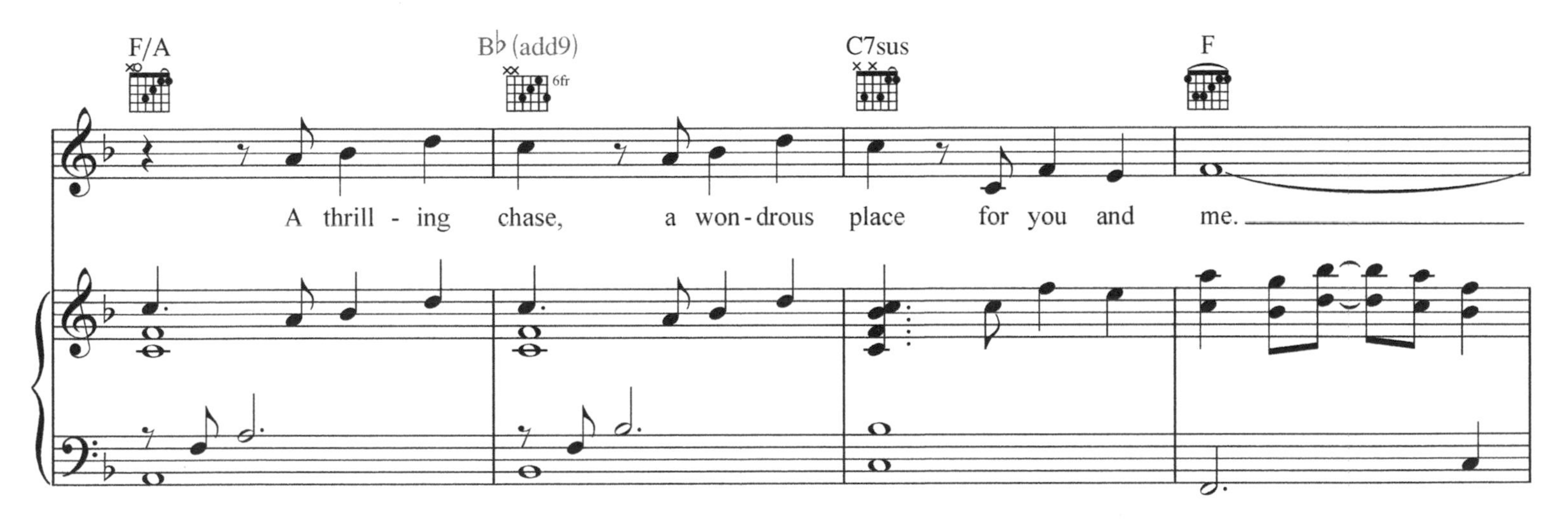
F/A
B♭(add9)
6fr
C7sus
F
A thrill - ing chase, a won - drous place for you and me.

rit.

YOU'VE GOT A FRIEND IN ME

from Walt Disney's TOY STORY

Music and Lyrics by
RANDY NEWMAN

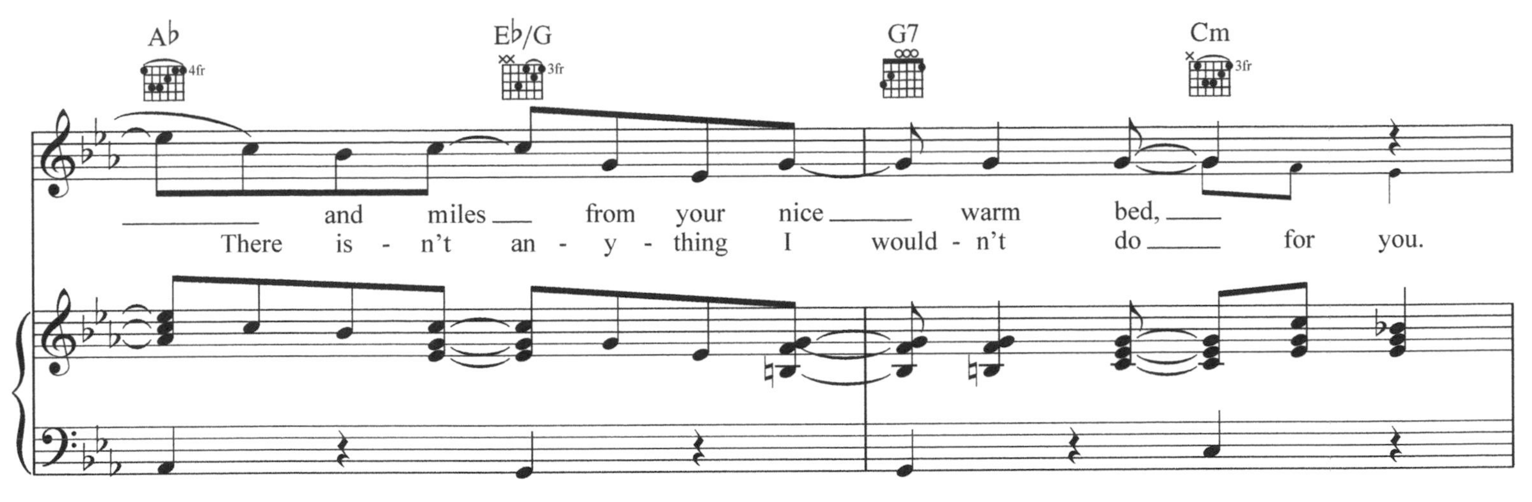
A♭
E♭/G
G7
Cm
and miles from your nice warm bed,
There is - n't an - y - thing I would - n't do for you.

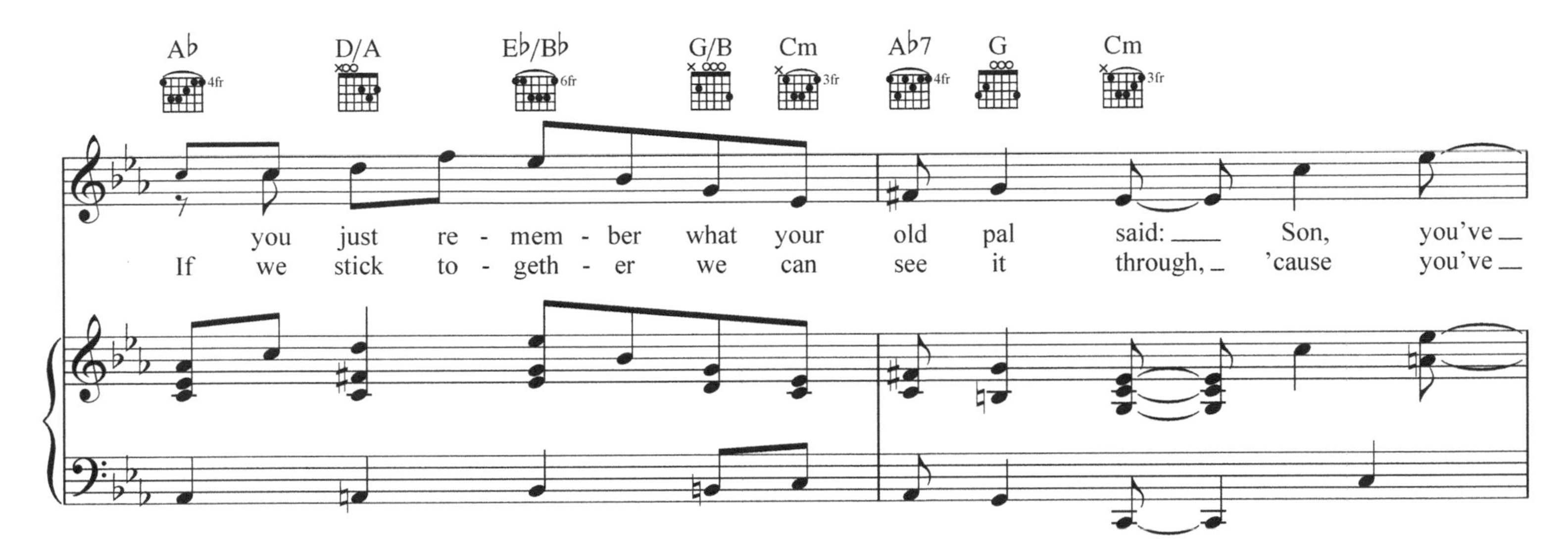
A♭
D/A
E♭/B♭
G/B
Cm
A♭7
G
Cm
you just re - mem - ber what your old pal said: Son, you've
If we stick to - geth - er we can see it through, 'cause you've

F7
B♭7
E♭
C7
F7
B♭7
got a friend in me. Yeah, you've got a friend in me.
got a friend in me. Yeah, you've got a friend in me.

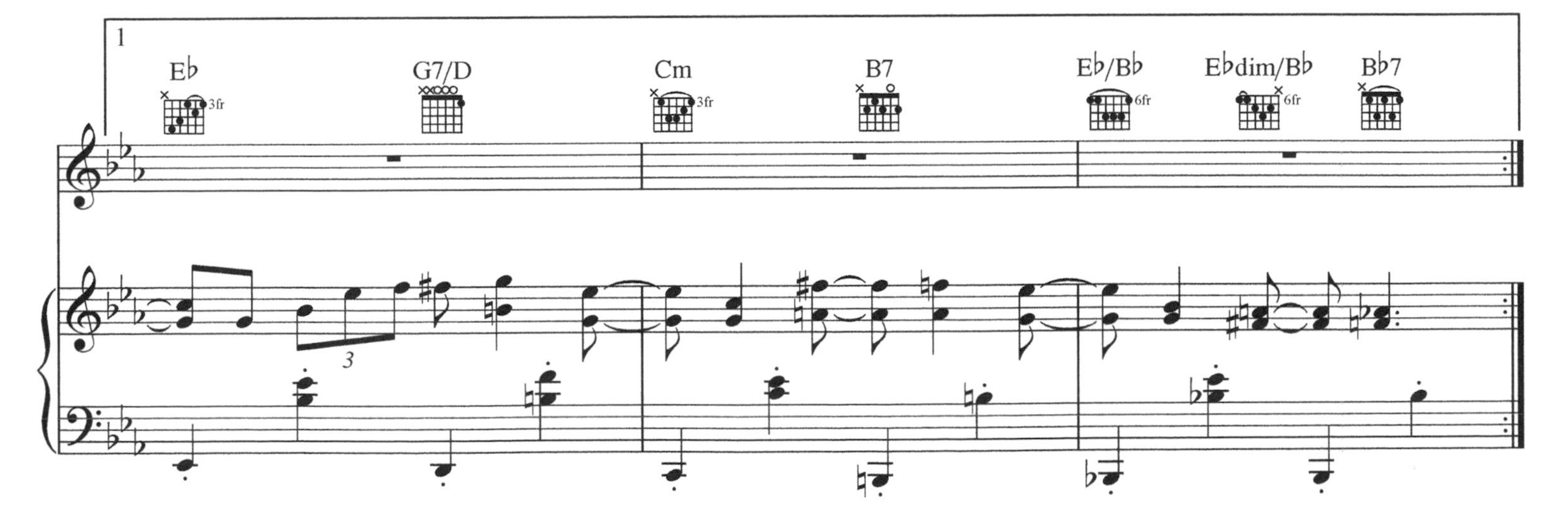
1
E♭
G7/D
Cm
B7
E♭/B♭
E♭dim/B♭
B♭7

2
E♭ E♭maj7 E♭7 A♭ D
3fr 3fr 4fr
Now, some oth - er folks might be a lit - tle bit smart-er than I am,

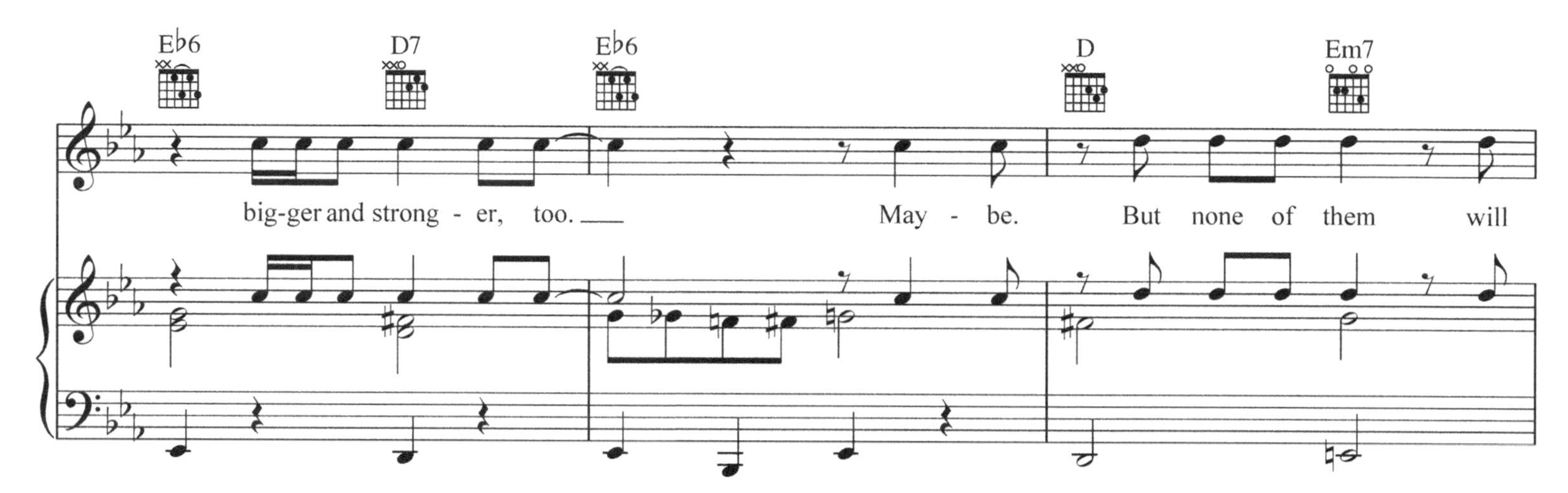
E♭6 D7 E♭6 D Em7
big-ger and strong - er, too. May - be. But none of them will

Fdim7 D/F♯ Gm C7 Fm B♭7
3fr
ev - er love you the way I do, just me and you, boy.

E♭ B♭7♯5 E♭7 A♭ Adim7
3fr 6fr 4fr
And as the years go by, our friend - ship will nev - er die.

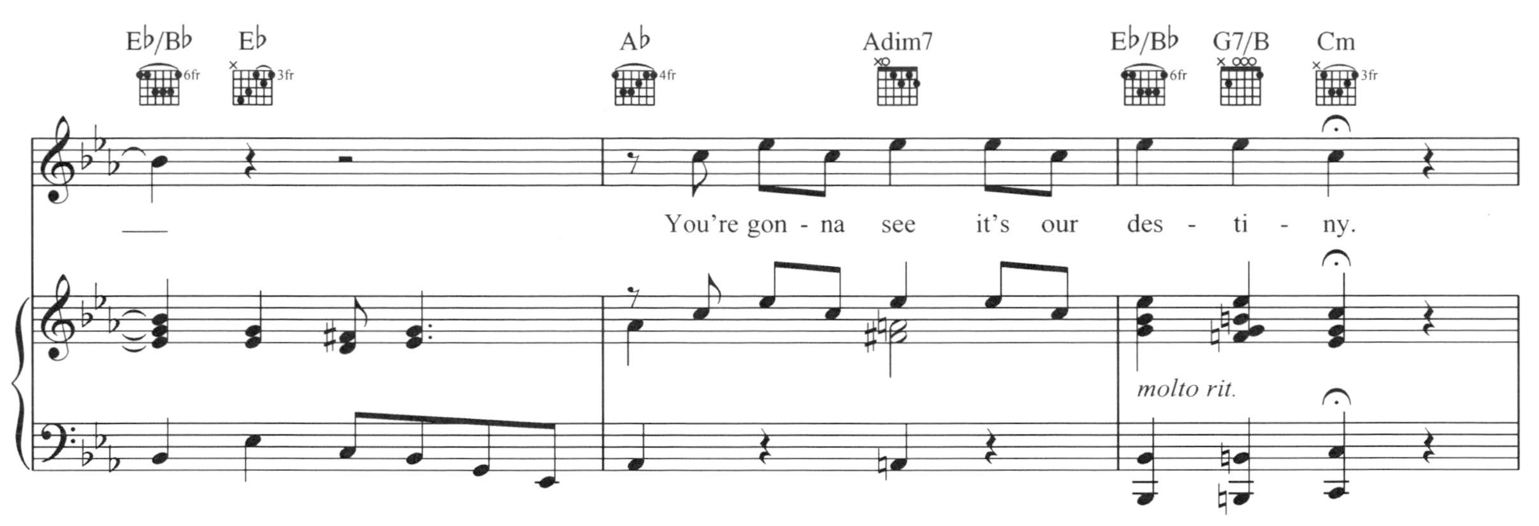
E♭/B♭
E♭
A♭
Adim7
E♭/B♭
G7/B
Cm
You're gon - na see it's our des - ti - ny.
molto rit.

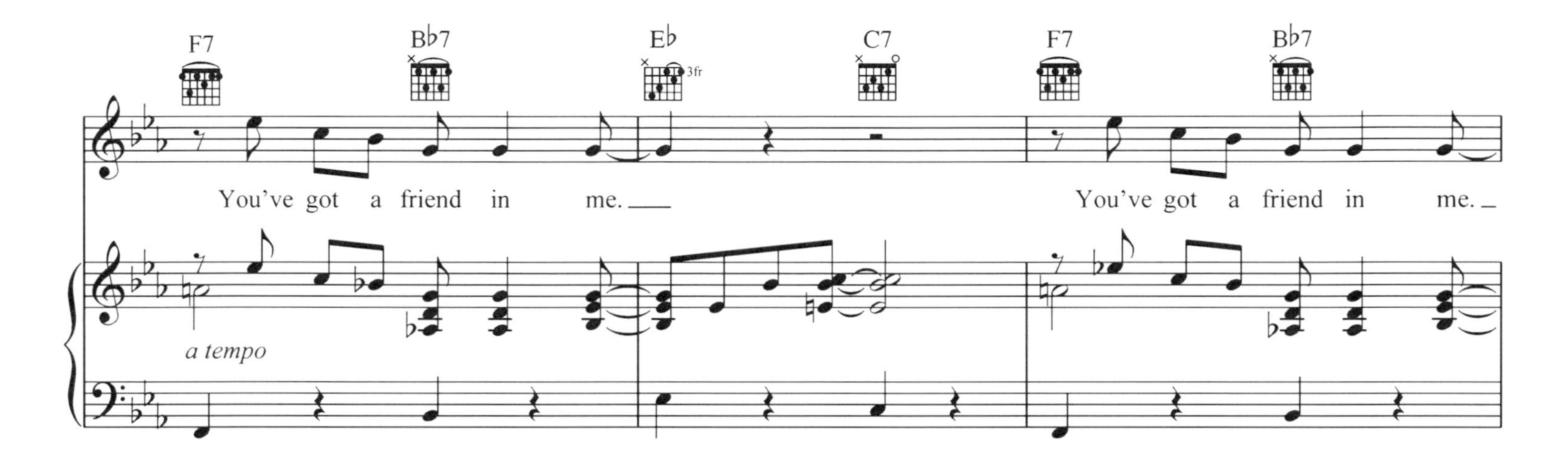
F7
B♭7
E♭
C7
F7
B♭7
You've got a friend in me.
You've got a friend in me.
a tempo

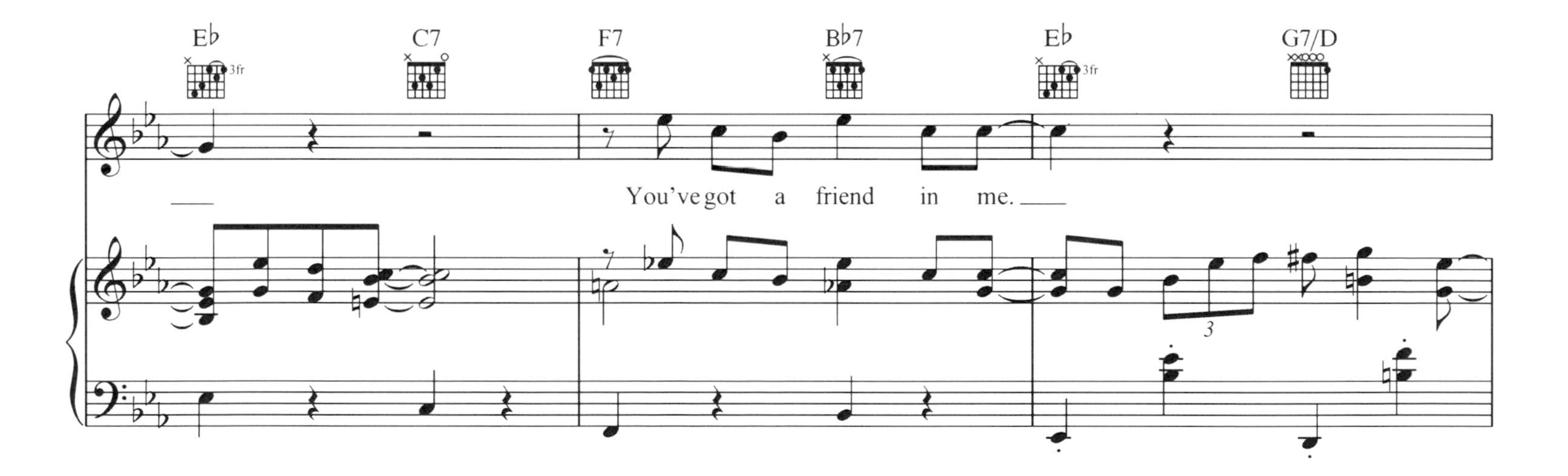
E♭
C7
F7
B♭7
E♭
G7/D
You've got a friend in me.

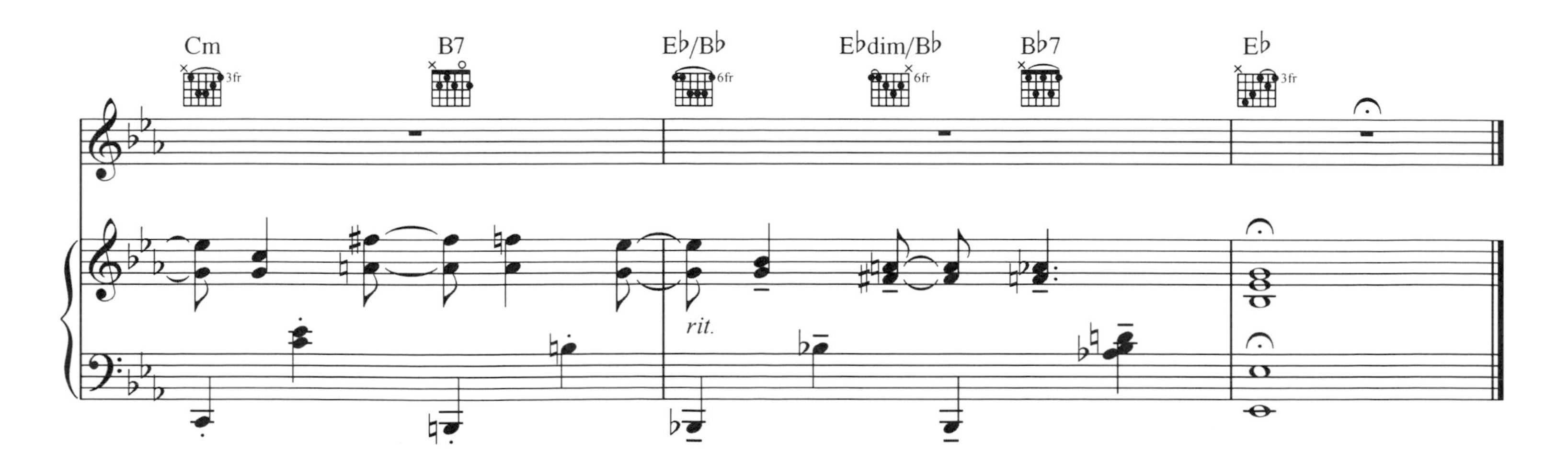
Cm
B7
E♭/B♭
E♭dim/B♭
B♭7
E♭
rit.

THE ULTIMATE SONGBOOKS

HAL•LEONARD®

PIANO PLAY-ALONG

These great songbook/audio packs come with our standard arrangements for piano and voice with guitar chord frames plus audio. The audio includes a full performance of each song, as well as a second track without the piano part so you can play "lead" with the band!

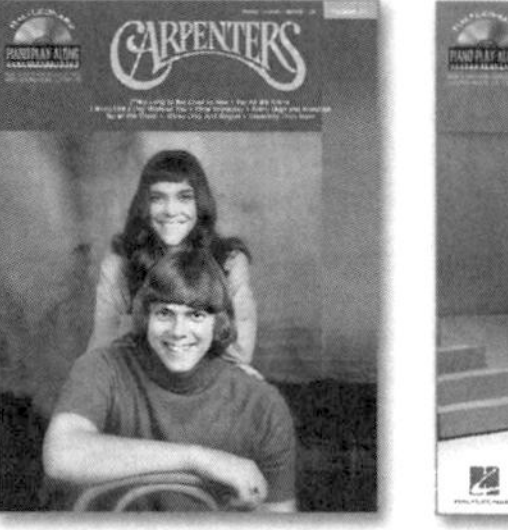

BOOK/CD PACKS

1. **Movie Music** 00311072 .... $14.95
7. **Love Songs** 00311078 .... $14.95
12. **Christmas Favorites** 00311137 .... $15.95
15. **Favorite Standards** 00311146 .... $14.95
27. **Andrew Lloyd Webber Greats** 00311179 .... $14.95
28. **Lennon & McCartney** 00311180 .... $14.95
44. **Frank Sinatra – Popular Hits** 00311277 .... $14.95
71. **George Gershwin** 00102687 .... $24.99
77. **Elton John Favorites** 00311884 .... $14.99
78. **Eric Clapton** 00311885 .... $14.99
81. **Josh Groban** 00311901 .... $14.99
82. **Lionel Richie** 00311902 .... $14.99
86. **Barry Manilow** 00311935 .... $14.99
87. **Patsy Cline** 00311936 .... $14.99
90. **Irish Favorites** 00311969 .... $14.99
92. **Disney Favorites** 00311973 .... $14.99
97. **Great Classical Themes** 00312020 .... $14.99
98. **Christmas Cheer** 00312021 .... $14.99
105. **Bee Gees** 00312055 .... $14.99
106. **Carole King** 00312056 .... $14.99
107. **Bob Dylan** 00312057 .... $16.99
108. **Simon & Garfunkel** 00312058 .... $16.99
114. **Motown** 00312176 .... $14.99
115. **John Denver** 00312249 .... $14.99
123. **Chris Tomlin** 00312563 .... $14.99
125. **Katy Perry** 00109373 .... $14.99

BOOKS/ONLINE AUDIO

5. **Disney** 00311076 .... $14.99
8. **The Piano Guys – Uncharted** 00202549 .... $24.99
9. **The Piano Guys – Christmas Together** 00259567 .... $24.99
16. **Coldplay** 00316506 .... $17.99
20. **La La Land** 00241591 .... $19.99
24. **Les Misérables** 00311169 .... $14.99
25. **The Sound of Music** 00311175 .... $15.99
30. **Elton John Hits** 00311182 .... $16.99
31. **Carpenters** 00311183 .... $17.99
32. **Adele** 00156222 .... $24.99
33. **Peanuts™** 00311227 .... $17.99
34. **A Charlie Brown Christmas** 00311228 .... $16.99
46. **Wicked** 00311317 .... $17.99
62. **Billy Joel Hits** 00311465 .... $14.99
65. **Casting Crowns** 00311494 .... $14.99
69. **Pirates of the Caribbean** 00311807 .... $17.99
72. **Van Morrison** 00103053 .... $16.99
73. **Mamma Mia! – The Movie** 00311831 .... $17.99
76. **Pride & Prejudice** 00311862 .... $15.99
83. **Phantom of the Opera** 00311903 .... $16.99
113. **Queen** 00312164 .... $16.99
117. **Alicia Keys** 00312306 .... $17.99
126. **Bruno Mars** 00123121 .... $19.99
127. **Star Wars** 00110282 .... $16.99
128 **Frozen** 00126480 .... $16.99
130. **West Side Story** 00130738 .... $14.99
131. **The Piano Guys – Wonders** 00141503 (Contains backing tracks only) $24.99

7777 W. Bluemound Rd. P.O. Box 13819 Milwaukee, WI 53213

Order online from your favorite music retailer at
halleonard.com

Prices, contents and availability subject to change without notice

0322
276